A CENTURY OF SPORT

CELEBRATION INSPIRATION ASPIRATION

STAN ADDICOTT

y Olfa

First impression: 2022

© Copyright Stan Addicott and Y Lolfa Cyf., 2022

The contents of this book are subject to copyright, and may not be reproduced by any means, mechanical or electronic, without the prior, written consent of the publishers.

Cover design: Y Lolfa

ISBN: 978-1-80099-289-4

Published and printed in Wales
on paper from well-maintained forests by
Y Lolfa Cyf., Talybont, Ceredigion SY24 5HE
website www.ylolfa.com
e-mail ylolfa@ylolfa.com
tel 01970 832 304

Table of contents

7	FOREWORD
10	PREFACE
12	INTRODUCTION
14	CHAPTER ONE
	The 1920s and 1930s: Getting set and making a mark
31	CHAPTER TWO
	The 1940s and 50s: Demise and rise
50	CHAPTER THREE
	The 1960s and 70s: 'Swinging and singing'
76	CHAPTER FOUR
	The 1980s and 90s: A leap forward, partnerships and progress
112	CHAPTER FIVE
	The 2000s and 2010s: New Millennium and milestone ahead
147	OTHER SPORTING DEVELOPMENTS
	Staff participation, PGCE (PE), Sports Science, Sport and the Media
155	CONCLUSION
157	ABBREVIATIONS
160	APPENDIX
166	NOTES
172	BIBLIOGRAPHY
174	ILLUSTRATIONS
175	ACKNOWLEDGEMENTS

Foreword

In 2020, we celebrated the centenary of Swansea University, and reflected not only upon one hundred years of growth and progress for our institution, but also upon the development of a rich heritage, forged by our community. Sport is a distinctive feature of that heritage, woven into our tapestry of tradition, and forming a significant part of the life of our University community from its earliest days.

The author of this book, Stan Addicott, served as a highly valued member of our staff community across four decades. This book is shaped by Stan's love for – and knowledge of – our institution, along with his own treasured memories of links with sports people and places from our University's earliest years. Within these pages, he has crafted a comprehensive picture of the development, nature and scope of sport at Swansea over the past century, set against the backdrop of the social and political events of the time.

He documents the inspiring sporting achievements of our students and alumni within our University, our local and regional community and on the international stage. This book articulates the importance of sport for sport's sake, tracing the sheer pleasure and enjoyment of our participating staff and students, while outlining its many other benefits.

In our second century, our strategy for sport builds upon the proud sporting legacy charted within these pages, promoting activity at all levels – from introductory to high performance – and contributing to the health, leisure and wellbeing of our wider regional community.

PROFESSOR PAUL BOYLE
Vice-Chancellor, Swansea University
June 2022

"The past is never fully gone. It is absorbed into the present and the future. It stays to shape what we are and what we do."

– Australian Journey Gallery
National Museum of Australia, Canberra

Preface

THE ORIGINS OF UNIVERSITY SPORT can be traced back to the history of the universities of Oxford and Cambridge. It is recorded that an Oxford student was killed playing football as long ago as 1303. In the 16th century both Oxford and Cambridge prohibited football on sufferance of a fine of six shillings and eight pence at Cambridge and of twenty shillings and imprisonment at Oxford. [1] University sport as practised that long ago bore little resemblance to modern day sport but even sport as we now know it has existed in university life for over a century and a half.

Although the lifespan of Swansea University (founded in 1920) runs for only a fraction of the time of the existence of Oxbridge, in celebrating its centenary Swansea has a colourful picture of sport to present. Operating in a different age, Swansea's early students were thankfully spared the threat of the imposition of fines, incarcerations and prohibitions for playing sport. More so, during the 100 years of its existence the genesis and growth of sport at Swansea has largely been accompanied by encouragement, support and goodwill. It is the story of that rich development that this book attempts to relate.

Information has been garnered from the sources outlined below, and through personal experience. An effort is made

Preface

to describe and explain the nature and scope of Swansea University sport as a social institution, and to restore its personality, mind and spirit to life. There have been many outstanding team and individual achievements. Yet any team sport is more than its stars and only performs as well as all its members' play. Similarly, in individual sports 'no man (or woman) is an island' and success is never down to one person alone. There are always others who have contributed and participated along the way, in one form or another, some for sheer fun and enjoyment. Such is the case during the first hundred years of Swansea University.

Source material is drawn from student and national newspapers, memoirs, match reports, programmes, handbooks, government publications, annual University reports, interviews and publications on the social history of sport. It is not felt necessary to overload the text with a strict structure of references for without too much difficulty it should be possible to trace the archives and publications listed in the bibliography.

I hope you enjoy the read.

STAN ADDICOTT
May 2022

Introduction

THE ARRIVAL OF the centenary of Swansea University provides an opportunity to reflect, explore and provide insights into the nature and scope of sport, which has played a prominent part in the life of the University community.

In order to appreciate its character and place in the University setting, sport should be seen as encompassing a range of 'physical activity concepts'. These include physical education and recreation; exercise and health; strength and conditioning; performance and elite sport; games and sports science; competition and co-operation; participation and leisure, and training and fitness. These various strands will be referred to during the narrative. The physical, psychological, social and spiritual benefits associated with sport will also become apparent. Such benefits have deserved, and received, support in the form of enhanced facilities, scholarships, sponsorships and goodwill from both the University and local community. Diversity, inclusiveness, equality, leadership, achievements (including those of alumni), contributions to the community and partnerships with external organisations are discussed. Concerns surrounding student sport also feature, for excesses and over-indulgence are all part of the picture too.

The surrounding context affecting sport down the years is considered, including relevant national and local events, legislation, individuals and the growth of student numbers. Also, in referring to the broader context, some decade

Introduction

highlights have been randomly selected recalling political, social, sporting events and personalities. This is done in an attempt to illustrate the distinctive moods and colour of various periods in time (whilst bearing in mind that there are no clear breaks between epochs) to allow some reminiscence. To further enable this with some perspective and order, an effort will be made to relate this snapshot story of University sport by picturing the 100 years in five blocks of twenty-year periods. For ease of expression what was the 'college' will be referred to throughout as the 'University' whilst acknowledging that the institution was originally named University College Swansea (as part of the University of Wales) before undergoing a name change to the University of Wales Swansea in 1996 and another to Swansea University in 2007. Also, the main focus will be on Singleton while recognising the opening of the superb new Bay Campus in 2015.

This work is not intended to be a definitive catalogue of sports, events and achievements. It is meant to offer a flavour of sport during the 100 years. Restrictions on space for words and images and limited time for research have inevitably left some sources untapped. If any person or contribution deserving of mention is left out, it is not intentional; and if any sport is felt to be worthy of more attention than it receives here, then forgive me. The availability of student newspaper sources and accounts varies considerably according to the popularity of particular sports, the enthusiasm of contributors and their writing styles. Some facts and opinions will undoubtedly be challenged, yet if further hours of nostalgic, friendly or heated discussion are provoked then so much the better! It is inevitable too that the treatment of more recent years in the University's sporting affairs is unashamedly more personal and detailed, reflecting the many happy and valued occasions that I myself was fortunate to spend with students and staff.

CHAPTER ONE

The 1920s and 1930s: getting set and making a mark

Swansea University was founded in 1920. It enjoys a unique and distinct location within the greenery of the Singleton Estate, in close proximity to the beach and the stunning views of Swansea Bay. The beautiful Gower coastline lies to the west and there is easy access to the city centre towards the east. For those with an eye for sport, near the University can be found the famous St Helen's sports ground, a hallowed venue for club, county, international rugby and cricket. Closer to the city centre was the Vetch Field (now a commemorative garden space since the building of the Liberty Stadium (now the Swansea.com Stadium) where Swansea Town (now City) played English league football and Wales hosted international matches. Four miles to the west of the University's Singleton site sits the old fishing village of Mumbles with its rowing and sailing clubs where regular summer regattas are held. During the Twenties, the southwest Wales hinterland consisted of river valleys, industrial villages and towns with their sports clubs and grammar schools. Swansea had a strong attachment to these areas and was seen to be in an advantageous place for students to enjoy both study and sport. Indeed, with a little

The 1920s and 1930s

stretch of the imagination it might be claimed that Swansea University was founded on sport. The ceremonial laying of the foundation stone by King George V on 19th July 1920 took place in "... the picturesque parkland setting of the archery lawn". [1] Archery had been a leisure pursuit of the Vivian family when they owned the Singleton Estate. However, in order not to let imagination or presumption run too free, and to offer respect for the founding fathers and their academic vision, some caution must prevail. Nevertheless, Swansea University was to build alongside its excellent academic reputation an enviable tradition of sport, for which its students, alumni, local community and the country can take some pride. It is the story of this heritage that the following narrative attempts to reveal.

A short review of student sport before 1920 will afford some context. The roots of university sport can be traced back to the histories of Oxford and Cambridge universities where, during the latter part of the 19th century, the ethos of public school sporting development was embraced. Oxbridge had an effect on other universities that followed similar patterns. However, in 1902 a Royal Commission examining the physical fitness of the nation listed amongst its findings: "the completely unsatisfactory provision of physical training in the universities". (2) Nevertheless, during the early part of the 20th century sports clubs sprang up in universities such as Durham, Manchester, Leeds, Bangor, Aberystwyth and Cardiff and a feeling emerged that an association was necessary to promote the different sports. In 1919 an Inter Varsity Athletics Board (IVAB), later to become the Universities Athletic Union (UAU) in 1931, was formed. IVAB recorded its opinion on the status of sport in universities. It considered that sporting facilities were inadequate in most universities and made recommendations and observations such as that students should have control over their athletic affairs and that Wednesday should become the recognised mid-week afternoon for sport in addition to Saturday.

IVAB (under a future variety of names) played a notable part in the development of sport in universities especially through the organisation of competitions, championships and representative teams. A sister association for women called the Women's Inter Varsity Board (WIVAB) was formed in 1923 and merged with the UAU in 1979. It is apt to record that IVAB (or BUCS as it is now known) celebrated its own centenary year twelve months prior to Swansea.

On a wider front, the ending of the First World War (1914-1918) soon saw the onset of the 'Roaring Twenties', a term associated with prosperity and consumerism. However, it was to become a decade of contrasts. Hope, liberation and a growing economy gave way to a period of depression, deflation and decline. From a decade that began with such a 'boom' the Twenties ended in 'bust'. Both the war and the contrasting features of the economy affected sport.

The loss of sportsmen during the conflict undoubtedly cast a shadow over activities. However, many who had served in the armed forces returned with a new or stronger passion for organised sport, for it had been actively encouraged in the army, played at every camp and even at the Front. On the other hand, women who enjoyed playing football for munitions factory teams were deprived of further opportunities when their workplaces closed and the Football Association (FA) banned them from playing in the stadia of professional clubs in 1921. Despite the attraction of large crowds (or perhaps because of it, as a possible threat to the reviving men's game) it was claimed that football was: "a most unsuitable game, too much for a woman's frame".

On the international scene, Olympic sport gained momentum with three Olympiads held at Antwerp (1920), Paris (1924) and Amsterdam (1928). Sporting heroes of the time were worshipped such as athletes Eric Liddell and Harold Abrahams; cricketers Jack Hobbs and Harold Larwood; footballer Dixie Dean and tennis player Kitty Godfrey.

In Wales during the short-lived economic boom, football thrived with six teams in the English Football League and Cardiff City won the FA cup in 1927. For rugby, although Wales won the Home Nations Championship in 1922, it was an inauspicious decade as the game suffered from the departure of many of its players to rugby league and the search for more stable employment in England. Cricket received a boost with the acceptance of Glamorgan into the first-class counties championship in 1921 and further interest was developed through the use of 'out grounds' like St Helen's in Swansea and the formation of a number of regional cricket leagues.

Big crowds followed teams like Cardiff City and international rugby matches involving Wales, when the fervent singing of hymns and the Welsh national anthem fuelled the atmosphere and acted as a "challenge to the enemy and a prayer for their overthrow". Crowds benefited hoteliers, publicans and newspaper sales. Betting and gambling were a great temptation, particularly for the working class. Greyhound and horse racing, Powderhall athletics and the football pools attracted those keen on a 'flutter'. However, as the depression enveloped the country, payment for access to sporting events grew more difficult. Attendances dropped (only 15,000 watched the Wales versus France rugby international at St Helen's in 1927) and many clubs had to borrow and beg for resources while some collapsed. [3]

Within this wider context Swansea University sport was 'getting set' for its initial cohort of eighty-nine students in 1920-21. At the end of its first academic year Ivor Evans, president of the Students Representative Council (SRC), was quoted as saying: "A good start has been made in sport. The rugger and football have nearly always played against big odds ... the hockey, thanks to its women students, is now in good swing". [4] One G Edwards helped to provide the swing and was elected women's captain for the following year. As there were only eight women students in the initial student intake, hockey did not appear until 1921-22. Ivor Evans was one of many who had served in the armed forces in World War 1 and had returned with enthusiasm for organised sport. The rugby team, under their first captain, I Williams, won its debut match against Llanelly Old Boys on 23rd October but it was the only recorded victory from twelve games. The football team played nine matches and men's hockey ten. [5]

The academic year 1921-22 was significant due to the founding of the Central Athletics Board (CAB), a student body formed to organise sport and co-ordinate the early established rugby, football, hockey (men and women), tennis (men and women) and cricket clubs. A harriers club was active from 1922 and a women's netball club from 1924-5. The awarding of 'colours' was established through the CAB that allowed the colours blazer to be worn in recognition of half colours and caps were awarded for full colours. Green and white became the traditional hue of playing kits and awards as well as other university paraphernalia. This choice of colour has stood the test of time to the present day for sport, despite the rebranding of the University in 2007 and an official change to blue.

A feature of the 1920s was Swansea's participation in the University of Wales Inter Collegiate Week (inter-coll). Existing programmes from 1923/24/25 show the organisation undertaken in Swansea during February and early March during the latter year. There were sporting and cultural events while hosting Bangor, Aberystwyth and Cardiff. Apart from the sports matches, social functions took place including dances, dinners, concerts, whist drives, drama and a debate. Venues such as the Exchange Restaurant, Empire Theatre, Patti Pavilion and the College refectory were used. Programmes also stated train travel times to and from the host venue for the participating colleges. [6]

Other opponents for the sports teams came from south Wales colleges, clubs and teams across the border from the Midlands and the West Country. The fortunes of the various

The 1920s and 1930s

University clubs fluctuated with football showing a "lack of interest" while recording three wins out of nineteen matches (1924-25) but becoming the "surprise team of the year" (1925-26) when they registered their first victory in inter-coll against Aberystwyth. Help with refereeing for the club was forthcoming from metallurgy staff members Mr G A Tandy and Dr McNair indicating an early interest shown by staff in student sport.

W R Mandel captained men's hockey in 1923-24 and in 1926 the club was regarded as the most successful team in the University winning two out of three inter-college games while showing an "excellent team spirit". By 1927-28 the 1st XI had a strong fixture list but intentions of fielding a 2nd XI were thwarted as: "… officials showed more aptitude in arranging fixtures than fulfilling them". The rugby club grew sufficiently to field a 2nd XV in 1925 and were well represented by eight players in a newly-formed University of Wales (UW) team that toured Ireland towards the end of the decade. The women's hockey team earned their first victory in inter-coll week against Aberystwyth in 1923 and followed this by beating Cardiff in 1924 and 1925.

Four students stood out for their achievements in University and more so after graduating. English student and rugby player Watcyn Thomas from Llanelli, was described as "an awesome colossus" on campus. He featured in a *Dawn* cartoon, captained the University team and played fourteen times for Wales, leading his country to a first victory over England at Twickenham. In March 1927 he wrote to the college registrar requesting: "… permission to absent myself from College duties … and to be excused sitting the Lent terminal examinations" for he had been selected to play for Wales against Ireland in Dublin and his revision time would be affected. [7] His leave of absence was granted, this being the first instance of an elite athlete requiring support in an effort to balance his academic work with top class sport.

Idwal Rees and Claude Davey were two other outstanding rugby players who also played for Swansea RFC and went on to represent and captain their country. The versatile Rees also won two blues at Cambridge and his professional career in education saw a long tenure as headmaster of Cowbridge Grammar School. During his retirement he served on the University Council and this writer enjoyed his company on an appointments board and when he visited Sketty Lane. The all-action Davey was thought by some to be the original exponent of 'crash'-tackling. Born in Garnant, he played twenty-three times for Wales and lived until the ripe old age of ninety-two. A lesser-known individual, J D B 'Jack' Williams, played in the men's hockey team and sat on the CAB. He became a physics teacher at Mountain Ash Grammar School. Williams later gave sterling service to Welsh schools and senior athletics as an administrator and was the chief officer in that sport and executive at HQ during the Empire (now Commonwealth) Games in Cardiff in 1958. He received an Award of Honour from the Welsh Amateur Athletics Association.

Despite the interest and enthusiasm shown for sport in the universities the provision of facilities and specialist staff was slow nationally and locally. Swansea had no facilities of its own during the Twenties. Singleton Park, St Helen's, the Vetch Field, the Training College, tennis courts at Victoria Park and those at a small memorial park in Sketty, along with the Glanmor Central School netball court were amongst the 'home' venues.

In 1926, at the Congress of British Empire Universities, the Vice-Chancellor (VC) of Liverpool University announced that: "Our British Universities must provide no longer a one-sided, but an all-round education directed at the due development of body and mind alike." There was support from the VC of Birmingham University who claimed that universities should: "... affirm the principle that we are responsible for the physical welfare of our students as well as their intellectual and moral welfare." [8] Although these sentiments were agreed in principle, when the University Grants Committee (UGC) visited Swansea in 1929 there was dismay shown at the lack of recreational resources available for students. However, a much brighter picture was seen during a subsequent visit early in the next decade. [9]

The 1930s

THE THIRTIES were consumed by an economic downfall known as the Great Depression. Its effects were felt throughout Britain, more so in areas of heavy industry like south Wales. It became a decade of mass poverty, unemployment, dole queues and soup kitchens. Ironically, it was also a time of commercial and consumer development as well as economic misery. Factories in the Midlands and the South of England engaged in the mass production of cars, radios and other consumer goods. This contrasted with southeast Wales which was largely dependent on a ravaged coal industry. Although there was also a beneficial proliferation of new technologies such as international aviation, radio and film, it was also a time of violent extremism. The rise of authoritarian governments in some European countries like Germany and Italy fuelled the gathering storm of world war that eventually broke out in 1939 and took over the first half of the 1940s. All this has led to the period being described as a "nadir in human affairs".

Sport played a part in keeping up the spirit and self-esteem of the population, including the unemployed. International sports figures such as cricketers Don Bradman, Wally Hammond, Len Hutton; tennis player Fred Perry; boxers Joe Louis and Tommy Farr, and athlete Jesse Owens were widely acclaimed. As in the previous decade, those who could afford to travel and attend matches found themselves part of huge crowds when supporting rugby or football at Murrayfield, Twickenham and Wembley. Welsh supporters continued to display their patriotism through the singing of hymns and the wearing of daffodils and leeks. However, many fans were dismayed although not resentful, of the continued flow of sportsmen from the Valleys to the greener pastures of England in search of employment and to play professionally. It was estimated that approximately 900 Welsh rugby players, including seventy internationals, swapped codes between 1919 and1939 bringing benefits to the rugby league game. These included University alumnus Willie Davies, more of whom later.

At the more local level, opportunities to participate only prevailed under some difficult conditions with regard to the provision and availability of facilities, equipment and playing kit. There was a reliance on benevolent landowners and companies as well as miners' welfare schemes. Football and rugby were played in a spirit that reflected the tough physical life of the working class communities that taught young players "what it meant to be a man". For the less physically inclined pub and club sports remained popular including billiards, snooker, darts and table tennis while outdoors quoits and pigeon racing attracted interest [1]

A natural source of students for the universities was of course the schools, and during the decade a wider scope in the physical education curriculum gradually saw a place for traditional popular team sports as an alternative to the more formalised system of drill. The grammar schools tended to promote rugby while elementary schools favoured football. Successful teams were supported by the wider townspeople and a crowd of 20,000 spectators cheered on the Swansea schoolboys when they won the English Schools Shield final at the Vetch Field in 1939.

Swansea students experienced much of the above when playing against opposition from Valley clubs but it was from wider influences that a big step forward was taken to improve the future of University sport. Sport and physical recreation benefited from government concerns about the nation's health and morale. Progressive thoughts regarding school physical education emanated from the foundation of Carnegie (1933) and Loughborough (1936) colleges. Organisations like the CCPR, NPFA, Keep Fit Movement, Women's League of Health and Beauty and the YHA all played a part. European youth movements and fitness campaigns, and the poor performance of Great Britain in the 1936 Berlin Olympics (accompanied by the glorification of German successes) all influenced opinion. The UGC Quinquennial Report (1929-34) and agitation from the National Union of Students (NUS) for better facilities saw local action. The King George V Jubilee Trust, the Physical Recreation Act and the National Advisory Council for Physical Fitness all impacted on Swansea University. Within this context there was significant expansion at Sketty Lane, a full-time staff appointment and a successful surge of interest in student sport during the decade.

In 1923 Swansea Corporation originally granted as part of the Singleton Estate fifteen acres of "swampy and un-reclaimed land" to be allocated for playing fields. However, because of the need to establish academic buildings it was not possible to immediately develop the recreational areas. Also, due to some misunderstanding about how the playing fields could be developed as part of the gift, nothing was done until the end of the decade. Alongside this projected development came a UGC grant of £4,000 in 1928 towards the approximate cost of £5,300 for a sports pavilion. The planning committee visited Birkbeck College in London and Bristol University to view their facilities and some similarities between all three are evident. Consequently, in May 1932 the chairman of the UGC officially opened the pavilion and some of the playing fields. As the original indoor sports facility at Sketty Lane, with its white painted exterior and 'classical' columns, it has proved to be a distinctive building for nearly 100 years, for thousands of travellers heading along from Mumbles towards the city centre. Its multi-purpose usage has seen it serve as a family home for the groundsman/caretaker, a meeting place for social occasions, an administrative base and service point for sports activities, a venue for lectures, together with changing rooms for teams. In the minds of some it can be compared to a 'castle or stronghold' for Swansea students preparing for battle against opponents in visiting university teams. By 1934 rugby, hockey, and two football pitches had been laid along with a netball court and four hard and three grass tennis courts. [2]

Two further significant developments occurred towards the end of the decade. These were the provision of new indoor facilities and the appointment of a full-time staff physical educationist. The UGC in keeping with the general mood for promoting physical culture provided a special capital grant of £3,500 towards the cost of building and equipping a gymnasium connected to the pavilion. It was completed in 1938. Also, in that year the University received a grant of £7,500 via the National Fitness Council and the UGC towards the cost of a swimming bath and two squash courts to be situated adjacent to the pavilion. The project encountered drainage problems that Dr Arthur Fordham, lecturer in the civil engineering department, was called upon successfully to resolve. It was not until the summer of 1940 that the bath was completed but it remained closed because of the war and the small number of students. It was not reopened until 1947. [3]

In 1938, Aberdare-born Vernon Jones, a graduate of Cardiff University who had trained as a physical education specialist at Carnegie College, was appointed as the University's first full-time 'instructor of physical training and swimming' in view of the: "urgent need for improving the physical education of the students". As a result, Swansea, along with the likes of Bristol, Leeds, Manchester and Liverpool had appointed a director of physical education (albeit under a variety of titles) before the outbreak of war.

What sort of benefits did the students gain from the new facilities? Following the opening ceremony of the pavilion, a cricket match was played on the new square between a combined College Council and staff team against the students. The rugby field was 'christened' with a match between the University and the All Whites on 12th October 1932. 'Pendragon', writing in the *South Wales Evening Post* commented favourably on the future prospects of the new fields and complimented the groundsman Ken Harris when stating that: "... no one in Wales knows more about the laying out of pitches" which was fortunate as the playing fields site was "in reality a converted refuse dump". It was also reported that the match brought "into prominence some talent of high quality". Glyn Davies stood out for the students alongside Neath RFC players Redvers Davies (future University 1st XV captain) and Raynor Jones. The result was a draw with one try apiece. [4] A return match was played at St Helen's in the following April which again ended in a draw. Pendragon reported once more that: "... carefree rugby was played by both sides but the Collegians were more enterprising fore and aft". He also stated that the match was to become an annual affair if a suggestion promoted by Principal Edwards was to be endorsed. [5] This may have been the sealing of a relationship between the 'town and gown' clubs that has blossomed down the years. Indeed, this was exemplified in 1935 when Swansea RFC defeated the touring New Zealand team with six University students (past, present and future) playing in the All Whites three-quarter line, namely Granville Davies, Ronnie Williams, Gwyn Griffiths, Claude Davey, W T H 'Willie' Davies and Haydn Tanner. The latter pair in addition to the already mentioned Davey had outstanding international careers. In the year of the famous win over the All Blacks, Tanner and Davies were still at Gowerton County School and Jack Manchester, captain of the defeated tourists at St Helen's, praised the Swansea team but added the postscript: "Please don't tell them at home that we were beaten by a pair of schoolboys". [6] In 1936-37 Tanner and Davies were playing for Swansea University and Wales.

Chemistry student Tanner went on to captain his country and play for the British Lions in 1938. It was said of him that: "Wales has produced few better players". Willie Davies later joined rugby league club Bradford Northern where he also enjoyed an outstanding career, representing Great Britain and touring Australia and New Zealand.

An interesting debate arose regarding the All Whites and University players in the seasons before the outbreak of war instigated by the writer Pendragon, who became critical of the All Whites' inconsistent form. Whilst praising the performances and significant contribution of Varsity men such as Watcyn Thomas, Gwili Jenkins, Gwyn Griffiths, Haydn Tanner, Willie Davies, Idwal Rees, Claude Davey and Ronnie Williams (who captained the All Whites and "led by magnificent example"), their inclusion brought consequences. Pendragon laid some of the blame for inconsistency on the fact that there was reliance on the University players. He pointed out that these men were obliged to turn out for the University, the UAU and other representative sides, including Wales, hence becoming 'unavailable' to Swansea RFC. He suggested that there should be a debate within the club about whether the All Whites might sacrifice the stars who appeared irregularly in order to field a more settled side. This theme was an interesting one for it was to raise its head again during the following decades – this time within the Varsity.

The 1930s proved to be a golden era for the rugby club with a number of student players and University teams gaining unprecedented success. The rugby team was especially successful in the UAU championship, winning five consecutive finals, losing in 1938, but winning again in the following year to make a total of six victories. Some players offered more than ability on the rugby field. Captain Sid Harris and Gwyn Griffiths, in turn, chaired the students' CAB. Harris also took part in athletics and boxing while Griffiths was a successful long jumper and University 100 yards sprint champion.

Hermas Evans acted as club secretary and in future years became principal of Gorseinon College. He was also a founder of the Wales Youth and Wales Students Rugby Unions as well as serving as president of the Welsh Rugby Union (WRU) in 1982-83. Another stalwart of the time Gwyn Roblin, a Wales schools' international, also went on to serve as president of the WRU in 1979-80, while Raynor Jones became chairman of the International Rugby Board (IRB).

Although rugby tended to be much in the spotlight in the 1930s, other previously established sports maintained their appeal and as the facilities developed and student numbers grew so did participation. By 1934 both men's and women's hockey, rugby, football, harriers and netball fielded second teams and there was men's cricket, and tennis too for men and women. In 1932 Barbara Kluge was a successful netball club captain. Playing standards improved in that club and largely due to the benefit of having its own court for practice and matches the team won the University of Wales (UW) championship for the first time in 1934. At the end of the decade Olwen Lloyd was elected captain but the players continued to bemoan the fact that a lack of netball teams in south Wales hindered the compilation of an attractive fixture list. There was a plea for more support for women's tennis in 1932 due to clashes with examination preparation. However, by 1935-36 when three grass and four new hard courts were ready, enthusiasm was such that there were thoughts of running a second team.

Regarding women's sporting activity, (a theme taken up throughout this narrative), long-standing attitudes suggesting that their participation in sport might harm, masculinise, or hinder their future marital and childbearing prospects were hard to erode. Although these attitudes prevailed nationally, they were recognised too by the University authorities for women's access to facilities was more restricted than that of the men. The University, with a view to pastoral care and decency timetabled access to the pavilion and playing fields.

This was reflected also in the traditional dress for women's sport consisting of kits fully covering the body with tunics, divided skirts and leggings. [7]

Returning to men's sports J B Williams captained the football team in 1930-31. He played for the UAU and was reserve for the Wales Amateur XI. In 1937-38 Ivor Isaac also represented the UAU on a tour of the Channel Islands. He was to bring his interest in sport to the University Playing Fields Committee (UPFC) in future years while serving on the academic staff. George Edwards earned selection for the Wales Amateur XI, Swansea Town and later enjoyed a glittering professional career. More will be written about him later.

New clubs were formed. In 1933 Tom Davies, part-time instructor and physical education lecturer, organised a gymnastics club: "to look after the physical needs of the students". Table tennis was started in the same year but had no suitable practice facility. This did not prevent Les Vivian from becoming West Glamorgan champion. By 1936 the women also had a team and although still lacking appropriate conditions, played their first season in the West Glamorgan league. A swimming club was formed by 1937-38 and sessions were held at the municipal baths. Trefor Evans was captain in the year that war broke out. Boxing had its followers and on the completion of the new gymnasium the club followed progressive practices in training and organised the UW championships at the Mannesman Hall in Dyfatty in 1939 where Vernon Jones acted as MC.

The harriers club, carrying a strong interest in cross-country running and athletics, became inter-college champions for the first time in 1932 under the captaincy of R G W Hopkins. The 1932 event was the tenth annual University of Wales Cross Country Championship and held in Swansea. A printed official programme (priced at 2d in 'old money') explains the arrangements for the day that included a description of the seven-and-a-half mile course, names of team members from each college, dinner at the Mackworth Hotel and a dance at the Arts building. Also mentioned in the programme are details of the University's rugby match against Cardiff to be played at St Helen's. The Cardiff team included Llew Rees who, on graduating, went on to Carnegie College and post-war became director of physical recreation at Bangor University in the early 1960s. He became a 'mentor' during my own university days at Bangor and his assistance was much appreciated when I captained the 1st XV. [8] By 1934 the harriers had twenty members and T H 'Ted' Prater was novice champion in that year. It was suggested that much of the success of the club was due to the attraction of the new pavilion as a headquarters. During the decade the athletics club competed in the Western Districts Athletics League and the harriers entered championships at Caerleon racecourse and Pontnewydd as well as UW and UAU events. W Anthony Rees was a staunch member and captain during the later years of the Thirties and a keen collector of the club's results, match reports and photographs. [9]

In June 1932 came the first organised intramural competition when a Sports Day was held at Sketty Lane. A programme of track, field and novelty events (such as potato races, flowerpot races and hockey ball dribbling for women) was scheduled to include students, staff and former students. The day involved competition between faculties, departments, teams and individuals. Cups, shields and other trophies (many still on view at the Sketty Lane Sports Centre) were provided by a variety of staff and the Old Students Association. R G W Hopkins won the Victor Ludorum and Sallie Rees the Victrix Ludorum. The second annual Sports Day (1933) was also a success and thanks for assistance were offered to Rowe Harding, international rugby player, future chair of the UPFC and respected judge. Gratitude was also expressed to other members of the University Council and staff for helping to organise and officiate on the day. The annual Sports

Day remained a feature of the sporting calendar and was instrumental in bringing students and staff together.

Student handbooks and diaries of the time published information on sport including details of the CAB, club sports officials, fixtures, records and finance. Amongst the University record holders were the aforementioned Willie Davies, who shared the 100 yards sprint record with a time of 10.2 seconds, recorded on the grass track at Sketty Lane in 1937. Towards the end of the decade, perhaps alluding to the more wary mood in wider society caused by the militarism stirring on the Continent, there were also appeals in the handbooks as follows: "Advice to freshers. Keep Fit! Make use of the Playing Fields and Pavilion. Watch out for organised classes of Swedish drill". [10]

Despite the political, economic and social milieu of the Thirties, the University had certainly been 'making a mark' in sport and looked well set for the future but the outbreak of war in 1939 was to alter that.

CHAPTER TWO

The 1940s and 50s: demise and rise

THE WAR YEARS (1939-1945) brought widespread air raids, evacuations, conscription and rationing. In an attempt to engender national spirit and lighten the mood many enjoyed popular music such as swing tunes played by Glenn Miller, other big bands and songs by 'Forces Favourite' Vera Lynn. Much of sport was severely disrupted, especially large spectator events. The 1940 and 1944 Olympics were cancelled. There was no Wimbledon, Five Nations Rugby or English first-class cricket. Some sport was encouraged at the more local level for fitness, diversion, morale, entertainment and charitable purposes. The armed forces promoted sport for the same reasons at home and abroad and fielded teams with exotic names like the Cairo Welsh Rugby XV.

The war had a numbing effect on Swansea and University sport. The true horror was brought home to Swansea by the Three-Day Blitz that changed the face of the town forever. University buildings and sports facilities were unscathed, but difficulties arose affecting student participation. There was a decline in student and staff numbers due mainly to entry into the armed forces. Travel restrictions were in place and Home Guard duties. UAU competitions were suspended. Food and clothing rationing affected both people's energy levels and the provision of playing kit. The fields and indoor facilities at Sketty Lane were requisitioned by the military for an army encampment of the 239 AA Battery of the Royal Artillery who were manning the emplacements by the Mumbles Road. Although the new swimming bath and squash courts were completed by 1940, they remained closed and used for storage. [1]

Yet sport did carry on and there were positives too that arose from the war years, albeit as unintended consequences. They will be referred to when discussing the post-war period. Despite the fact that there were less than 400 students during the early 1940s, sports clubs strove to fulfill their fixture lists. Glan Harries, CAB chairman stated in May 1941 that: "Some facilities offered students this year have been exceptionally poor ... We are still denied the use of our prized facilities ... No other Welsh college has suffered so severely in this respect ... Apologies must be offered to the first-year students for the bad impression". [2] Clubs were affected and when the rugby team lost the UW championship title for only the first time since 1926 it lamented that: "... organised training was impossible ... We eagerly await the day when, with the restoration of our much-prized playing fields, we will again enter the competition on an equal footing". [3]

The football club was unable to field a second team due to student Home Guard commitments but had an inspirational captain and top scorer in George Edwards. His future footballing career saw him play for Birmingham City and Cardiff City and earned him twelve caps for Wales. He was described as: "a rarity in his own footballing days, a player who attained a University degree". [4]

An inter-coll week was held at Swansea in February 1940, a highlight of which was the seven-and-three-quarter mile cross-country race from Sketty Lane, followed by an evening dinner at the Mackworth Hotel. However, during succeeding years the harriers had to cancel many away fixtures because

The 1940s and 50s

of expense and travelling difficulties. In 1941-42 the men's hockey team were UW champions under the captaincy of Gilbert Bennett who also led the College tennis team and UW teams in the same sports. He acted as president of the SRC, and years later, after teaching at Gowerton Grammar School, served on the staff of the University's education department. Bennett also became a BBC sports commentator and reporter. Women's hockey had little success during 1941-42 playing only eight games that included a defeat to Cardiff by 14-0. Both the University's men's and women's hockey teams suffered from a lack of practice facilities though the local education authority provided venues for matches. During the same session the netball club had "an enjoyable and successful season" but also lacked a practice court. In 1940 the boxing club was beaten by four bouts to two by Cardiff but during the following year stood firm in winning a return match by five bouts to three over eight weights. Table tennis was revived after a lapse of interest. [5]

Such was the picture of sport during the war years. There were enthusiastic attempts to keep going with smaller numbers, fewer facilities, a lack of equipment, funding and general resources – all mirroring war conditions nationally.

THE POST-WAR YEARS brought victory celebrations and a renewed social atmosphere with swing music making way for crooners like Al Jolson, Perry Como and Frank Sinatra and cinema-going became popular once more. Yet some consequences of war lingered on. Austerity, rationing, bombed sites and a need for better housing prevailed. Much of the country was heartened by the new Labour Government of 1945 whose policies included a welfare state, National Health Service, nationalisation of the heavy, manufacturing, transport and service industries as well as delivering the 1944 Education Act which was to help open up University entry.

It was a splendid time for sport with victory international matches played and attendances at major events were greater than ever. The 1948 London Olympics (known as the 'Austerity Games') had an opening ceremony attended by 85,000 people symbolising the rebirth of sport and the nation. In the same year, Glamorgan were county cricket champions under the captaincy of Wilfred Wooller, bringing another 'feel-good factor' closer to home.

The new hope and optimism of the post-war years were reflected in the universities. An interesting charity rugby match was arranged in 1947 at the Cardiff Arms Park by the aforementioned Swansea alumnus (and Wales rugby captain) Idwal Rees. It captured the mood of the time. By now Rees was headmaster of Cowbridge Grammar School. Using his connections in the game, he brought together Welsh international and University players. He selected an Idwal Rees XV that included future internationals like Bleddyn Williams and Cliff Davies to play against a University of Wales XV (Past and Present). The UW XV contained six players from Swansea. In the team were Haydn Tanner and Les Manfield from Mountain Ash, a Cardiff alumnus, former UW heavyweight boxing champion and holder of the DFC from his RAF war service. These were two of only four rugby players to appear for Wales before and after the war. Their careers had been deprived of seven years of international rugby. The proceeds of the game were shared between the Cardiff Royal Infirmary and the Cowbridge Grammar School War Memorial Fund. [6] The match reveals the willingness of players of the time to take part for worthy causes, the eagerness of pre-war international players to get started again and the involvement of students to provide an attractive fixture.

From 1945-50 student numbers in Swansea grew from just over 400 to more than 1,000 with ex-servicemen providing approximately half the student population annually during the second half of the decade. Members of staff returned too, and University sport was to benefit from some of the maturing experiences of their war. Former UAU football player Ivor

The 1940s and 50s

Isaac returned and became a professor and vice-principal. He was later to add his interest in sport to the UPFC. Ieuan Williams (although not a Swansea alumnus) was appointed to the University staff and became professor of adult and continuing education. He spent some of his war service in the RAF as a physical training instructor (PTI) at St Athan. He brought his expertise to chair the UPFC and played a significant part in overseeing the planning and building of the new Sports Centre during the 1970s. Vernon Jones returned to his post, sharing duties between the education department and physical recreation. He later stated that he: "... felt armed with the greater confidence and authority in my subject that the RAF had given me". His RAF experience included acting as a physical training instructor and in medical rehabilitation. He worked alongside outstanding serving sportsmen such as Dan Maskell of tennis fame, England cricketer R W V Robins and international footballers Raich Carter and Peter Doherty. [7]

Returning servicemen starting or resuming their studies also brought their experiences to University life and added leadership, colour, character, a respect for physical fitness and a social ethos to sport. One such returnee was Wyndham Davies who played cricket (1st XI captain in 1938-9) and hockey for the University pre-war. He joined the RAF in 1940 after graduating in English.

During his war service he played cricket several times at Lords for Fighter Command under former England captain Arthur Gilligan whom he befriended. He returned to Swansea in 1945-46 and qualified as a teacher in the education department. On completing his studies and armed with a testimonial from Gilligan, he took up his first post at Wellingborough Grammar School as English master and cricket coach. Davies later became a headmaster and a member of the MCC. However, one of his greatest sources of pride stemmed from a more local environment. When representing his home club Beaufort (Ebbw Vale) during the

University vacation he took all ten wickets for twelve runs in a match against Cardiff Strollers. [8]

The renewed vigour in the sports clubs was exemplified in rugby as the club won the UW cup in 1946-47 under the captaincy of W H Bowden. In that Swansea team was Alun Thomas who later played for Wales, the British and Irish Lions (1955) and managed the Lions on their unbeaten tour of South Africa in 1974. He also served as president of the WRU in 1985-86. Vivian Davies, who had seen war service in the Royal Navy, captained the 1st XV in 1948-49 when the club were again UW champions. However, a dilemma arose in the rugby club concerning team selection policy and whether returning servicemen who played for 'first-class' clubs (and not consistently for the University) should be selected for the prestigious UW cup matches in preference to those players more regularly available. Amongst these were the likes of future All Whites captain Len Davies and Howard Jones. A feature on the rugby club in *Crefft*, the student newspaper, stated that: "The rugby team is a many-headed monster, Janus-faced. There is one team for 'inter-colls' and one for the ordinary, presumably less glamorous games of Wednesday and Saturday week-in week-out. But always, captain Vivian Davies – and always playing as if King and Country and Destiny were involved in the tackle or in that breakthrough or in every dive at the bruising feet of forwards out for the ball or blood." [9] This was a worthy tribute to Davies whose son Russell T Davies in the 2010s was to become a celebrated screen writer, TV producer, BAFTA winner and whose work included 'Dr Who' and 'Queer as Folk'.

Another dilemma of a more personal nature was related to me as an example of the social mix of the time. Cliff David, a freshman student was a member of Viv Davies's rugby team. He was seventeen years old and playing in a team comprised of several mature ex-servicemen. While enjoying some post-match refreshment at a pub following an away

The 1940s and 50s

game, he was anxious about the fact that he was under the legal age for drinking. He was nervously worried that he might be dragged too far into the revelry shown by his more boisterous teammates and his age possibly being discovered by the law. As a 'callow youth' he was anxious that his future prospects might be compromised. Happily, David's concerns did not materialise and his future career in education saw him become a college principal and also a long-serving player and committee member of Aberavon RFC. Likewise, his captain that day, Viv Davies, enjoyed a successful career in education and gave sterling service to Swansea RFC.

By the end of the decade there was a revival in sports activity. I H Jenkins scored twenty-seven goals for the men's hockey club that was able to field a 2nd XI by 1948-49. 1st XI captain George Howitt also acted as CAB chairman. The women's team was successful under captain Rita Jones, and secretary Rhiannon Herbert organised seven away games and two at home for the1949-50 season. The netball club won the UW championship and had two players, Mary Davies and Cynthia Morris, in the UW side. Five football players including J E Budge, R J Williams, R Limbrick and K M Bishop and two boxers (Don Langley and Trevor Morgan) represented UW teams. Three rugby players were selected by the UAU. The UW swimming championships were held at the University pool for the first time and the principal and registrar presented the trophies. The squash and table tennis teams were also active. Two new clubs, basketball (with T C Green as captain elect) and badminton were affiliated to the CAB. However, although participation increased consistent performance was slow to follow for it was claimed at the end of the decade that in inter-coll matches: "... it would be difficult to find a bleaker year in the sporting life of coll."

During the 1949-50 session, efforts were made to revive the intramural sports competition so successfully inaugurated in 1932 yet not organised since 1938. A range of inter-faculty events was to be held culminating in a Sports (Athletics) Day at St Helen's as the Sketty Lane playing fields had not recovered since war time. Indoor events were to include a gymnastics display, squash, table tennis, badminton and pool activities including swimming, diving and water polo. The indoor programme went ahead but despite all preparations and the cancellation of lectures for the day, the vagaries of the weather determined that the outdoor sports had to be cancelled. Nevertheless, there were good signs that attempts were being made to bring students together in some healthy physical and social activity.

Towards the end of the decade there was a more organised approach to physical recreation with the timetabling of the gymnasium and swimming pool for beginner classes, staff, clubs and PGCE physical education sessions. However, while the indoor facilities were enjoying better usage, progress was slow with regard to bringing the playing fields back to pre-war standards. "No progress at Sports Fields" was the heading of a report on the front page of *Crefft*. There was criticism that the football, rugby and hockey pitches were unfit for play, causing difficulties in arranging home matches and that: "... the college sports grounds are still an eyesore with their scattered bricks and plentiful bumps and hollows". [10] However, tenders for £8,323 had been accepted to restore the fields to pre-war condition, work to be completed by 1950-51. It was stated that: "... the fields have been ploughed and the good seed scattered on the land. The contractors have done their job. Mother Nature must do the rest". Mother Nature did not act kindly, for an extremely wet summer in 1950 caused a sewer to burst on the playing fields leaving the grounds unfit and an apt quip – 'drain stopped play' – summed up the situation. [11]

Alongside the slow recovery of the playing fields, there were financial issues within the CAB that affected the cost of teams representing the University. It was decided that all hospitality for visiting teams and officials (with only one place for a host) should take place in the pavilion and not in local restaurants. Also, expenses were to be much tighter for students representing teams such as UW or UAU. The nature of University sport was showing its true amateur side. This issue was to be raised again in the coming years. However, although there had been some 'demise' during the decade a 'rise' was to follow.

The 1950s

THE FIFTIES saw some of the dreary legacies of the early post-war years continue but national events were soon to grip the nation's imagination. These were the Festival of Britain (1951), the Conquest of Everest (1953) and the Coronation (1953). Increased economic prosperity led to better standards of living. Seaside holidays and the advent of rock and roll music created a 'feel-good factor' for many that helped coin the term 'Fabulous Fifties'.

In sport there were record crowds for club matches, star performers and world champions. Many are memorialised in statues around the country including athlete Sir Roger Bannister, racing driver Sir Stirling Moss as well as Swansea's own illustrious football stars Ivor Allchurch and John Charles. The Monmouthshire town of Blaenavon honoured Welsh rugby player and Olympic medallist Ken Jones. However, there was no national single body to clearly represent sport. Sport was seen as a quintessentially voluntary activity and its organisation resembled something of a 'patchwork quilt'. Yet throughout the Forties and Fifties, organisations like the CCPR and the British Olympic Association (BOA) had the ear of the government.

In 1953 the NPFA, under its influential president the Duke of Edinburgh, lobbied strongly for more funding to develop facilities. There were government discussions on the constructive use of leisure time by young people and the encouragement of sport and recreational activities through the

Youth Service. The values of sport were re-assessed. It came to be seen as a 'common denominator', a means of fostering pride, cohesion and even a cure for crime and delinquency. A scientific approach was applied to developing skills and fitness with the emergence of circuit training and weight training. The Duke of Edinburgh Award Scheme was founded in 1956 and interest in Outward Bound and accessing the natural environment became more widespread. Changes in the school physical education curriculum, implemented by trained specialist teachers, encouraged team games. Access to youth clubs and YMCAs for young people introduced them to a broader range of activities not generally available in schools such as basketball, table tennis and snooker. These experiences were to benefit University sports clubs with the arrival of increased student numbers who had taken part in these games.

Despite the developments, during the early 1950s Britain's international prestige began to suffer. In the 1950 Football World Cup England lost to the less experienced USA team and suffered two heavy defeats against Hungary in 1953 and 1954. In 1950 the England cricket team lost a test match series at home to the West Indies for the first time, while in 1952 Great Britain gained only one gold medal at the Helsinki Olympics and that was won by a horse, Foxhunter, ridden by Colonel Harry Llewellyn.

Paradoxically, the Fifties were a fruitful time for Welsh sport. The Welsh rugby team won the Five Nations championship three times and shared it twice. In 1953 Wales beat the All Blacks with alumnus Alun Thomas in the side. In 1958 the Welsh football team reached the quarter-final of the World Cup in Sweden and in the same year the Empire (now Commonwealth) Games were successfully held in Cardiff with Wales winning eleven medals. Swansea alumnus J D B 'Jack' Williams was one of the key organisers of the Games.

As a result of some of the misgivings in British sport, an

The 1940s and 50s

investigation headed by Lord Wolfenden revealed how far behind the country was in provision for sport compared to the USA and other European countries. The Wolfenden Committee was established and produced a report 'Sport and the Community' in 1960. [1] This brought about changes in the government's attitude, making a long-term impact on the shape of British sport and had consequences for Wales and Swansea University that will be referred to as we go along.

At the University, student interest in sport gained momentum with encouragement for new students to make use of the facilities without the compulsion that might have been the case in the armed forces or at school. A growing number of clubs sought space for training and playing at the gymnasium.

Staffing was improved at the swimming pool with the appointment of John Palmer from Brynmawr as superintendent in 1951. He came from a post in Barking, Essex, and soon revised the opening hours, enabling better access and participation in swimming, lifesaving and personal survival classes. The water polo club were UW champions for the first time in 1958.

John was a committed Christian who lived into his 90s. He showed a care for both body and soul and his attitude to life is aptly summed up on a memorial bench situated outside the Pavilion, provided by his family. On it, a Bible-related inscription states that: "I have fought the good fight, I have finished the race, I have kept the faith." His more mischievous spirit was revealed when he recalled some of the daring antics of the students at the pool in the Fifties. At the deep end there was a springboard and a ten-feet high diving stage. However, there was also a steel roof rafter about five feet above the diving stage that offered a greater challenge in height. Chemistry student Bryn Gravenor, keen squash player, swimmer and diver, could not resist the temptation that the higher girder offered. He regularly scrambled up to

41

it to perform a perfect swallow dive into the water, defying health and safety regulations that were perhaps not as strictly observed during those days. In the Seventies Bryn returned to the University as professor of management science. He served too as a vice-principal. He was also a popular president of the student rugby club and was known at annual dinners to be able to transfer his swallow-diving prowess from the pool to the hotel bar onto which he would clamber up for a challenge known as 'bar diving'. This involved an outstretched take-off and landing into the arms of supporting students who had previously demonstrated the art – all accompanied by loud cheering!

In 1958 a new post was created at Sketty Lane where Bernard Warden was appointed to the position of gymnasium superintendent and instructor in physical recreation. He was a basketball enthusiast and promoted the values of weight training and good nutrition. This was to the delight of the CAB who commented that: "... after much bartering with the college authorities we are pleased to announce that we will have a full-time sports instructor to give coaching where needed and to supervise training".

Throughout the 1950s there were signs that the relationship between the SRC and CAB was not always cordial as growing tensions became evident. A recurring issue was that of finance. A cut in budget for the CAB threatened its activities in 1952 and in the following year it was stated that: "Coll sport is on the downfall. It is in fact on the bottom rung of the ladder". Finance was at the root of the matter and the SRC was criticised for spending £70 on an annual dinner function while the whole budget for sport for the year was £136. [2] As the decade progressed the CAB was getting stronger in expressing its vision and, led by enthusiastic chairmen in successive years, endeavoured to enhance its profile. By 1958-59 the back page of *Crefft* was reserved for sports clubs' reports. The position and relevance of CAB was to develop further during the next decade.

The 1940s and 50s

Women's sport was generally under-developed in society and this was reflected in the University. Only a few used the pool at reserved times. "The ladies showed little interest in College athletics" stated a *Crefft* report in 1952 when trying to gather support for an intramural sports day. "Apparently forty out of two hundred and six women regularly use the Playing Fields" was another claim. [3] Netball and hockey were popular in schools but in 1953 University teams found difficulty in fulfilling fixtures. Netball struggled for players with only four freshers turning up for trials. By 1956-57 greater support arrived (in accordance with the cyclical nature of student life) and the club became UW champions, a feat they repeated two years later when M Rickets and J Monday were prominent. In 1958-59 hockey improved under the captaincy of Barbara Davies who scored a hat-trick against BP Llandarcy. Dance sessions appealed as there was a good turn-out reported for folk and ballroom classes.

All was not well with men's sports. At the beginning of the 1950-51 session a shudder went through the rugby club and reverberated around the general body of students. "Howe to ban rugger stars" was the headline on the *Crefft* sports page. The new captain Frank Howe had declared that it was his intention not to select those players for UW and UAU championship games who were not available regularly for other matches. This echoed the dilemma already referred to at the end of the previous decade. Howe's decision was openly debated. Defeats were suffered in the championship, including one to Aberystwyth for whom a certain Carwyn James was prominent. Student Clive Gammon wrote to *Crefft* complaining about poor performances and termed the rugby team "Wooden Spoon Champions". [4] Howell Williams was captain in the following year and, to the relief of many, reversed Howe's decision, bringing back the stars. Amongst the stars of the era were Marsden Young and future All Whites captains Roy Sutton and Teifion Williams. The team promptly regained the UW title.

Bryan Richards served as captain in 1953. After graduating he won a blue at Cambridge, captained the All Whites and also played for London Welsh, the Barbarians and Wales. He taught at Rugby school and was a keen cricketer and golfer. In his later years he was registered blind but continued playing golf with the help of a sighted player and guide. He represented the England and Wales Blind Golf Association. His namesake, Ken Richards, won five caps for Wales in 1960-61 after graduating from Swansea, ironically taking the place of Bryan who won his only cap against France. He later played professionally for Salford rugby league club. Another Richards – Harry – played for the All Whites and the Scarlets before becoming a WRU referee.

A host of excellent players stood out in the 1950s and went on to contribute to the Welsh first-class rugby scene and beyond. The burly Ron Roberts (a freshman in 1953) played for Abertillery and became a regular spectator at Sketty Lane in the 1980s watching his son Mark playing hooker in the 1st XV. Mark followed in his father's footsteps, succeeding on the rugby field and later in the world of business. Bryan Mullins was a fleet-footed wing for the All Whites while Alan Prosser-Harries won a blue at Cambridge, as did Cardigan-born Dilwyn Davies at Oxford, and Jim Clifford played for the Barbarians. Others who made their marks included half-backs Ian James, Mansel Richards and Dai Harris. The latter became a leading coach in Welsh rugby during his time with Newbridge RFC. Amongst the forwards, Denny Jenkins, Perry Close and Hugh 'Bomber' Thomas were to the fore as well as the 'giant' Andy Chinn. 'Side-stepping' centre John Jeffreys was followed by his son Ian into University and All Whites rugby during the Eighties. In his post-University days, Ian enjoyed an academic career in sports science, becoming a professor at the University of South Wales. In 1958, under Dave Wooding's captaincy, Swansea won the UW championship and it was reported that there was a 'good spirit in the club' which no doubt pleased

The 1940s and 50s

club president Professor R 'Tug' Wilson and staff secretary Dr I G Evans.

At the beginning of the Fifties, the football club was fortunate to have two enthusiastic captains in Eddie Evans and John Gow. Evans (who served as chairman of CAB) and Gow both played for UW as did Graham Davies who also represented the British Universities against their German counterparts. John Gow retired early from playing due to injury and later became an outstanding referee in the Sixties and Seventies. He officiated in international matches and earned much respect for the way he handled tense derby games in the English League such as Arsenal and Tottenham, Liverpool against Everton and Manchester City versus Manchester United. John was a science master at Bishop Vaughan school in Swansea and, following retirement from refereeing, gave admirable service to Welsh and local football while training referees, regularly using the University facilities for his courses.

In 1952 the University football club entered the local Swansea Senior League for the first time, playing in Division One, but withdrew from the league in 1955 due to difficulties in fulfilling fixtures. Fortunes changed in 1957 when the club won the UW championship. A highlight of the 1959 season was a 1st XI match against Swansea Town who fielded eight first team players. The Swans weren't taking any chances. They need not have worried for the professionals won by eight goals to one with Brayley Reynolds scoring six and Welsh internationals Colin Webster and Graham Williams netting one each. Harry Griffiths, Norman Lawson and Roy Saunders were also in the Swans' line up and the latter two coached the University 1st XI in separate stints during the 1980s.

At the end of the 1959-60 season the University had four players, Alan Hopkins, Derek Lobley, Brian Lewis and George Renton in the UW team against the English Universities. Renton later became a regular member of the Wales Amateur XI, playing twenty-six times and captaining his country. He

45

was in the side that won the British Amateur Championship for the only time in 1967-68.

Men's hockey had to wait until the end of the Fifties for their best performance when, after winning the UW championship, they went on to reach the UAU final before losing to Nottingham with N C Harris their outstanding player. Men's tennis were UW champions in successive years early in the decade and also reached the UAU final under the leadership of B Perris.

The cricket club had high hopes of a good season with the availability of their facility at Sketty Lane in 1951. The 1st XI captain declared that: "The College has a first-class playing field under the able care of Mr Sanday the groundsman". Sanday, himself an accomplished cricketer, had succeeded his predecessor, Ken Harris, who sadly passed away as the playing fields were being re-instated.

The cricket club had use of its own pitch for the first time since the war. Particularly good use of it was made in the 1953-54 season when, under the captaincy of Richard Howard Thomas, the 1st XI won the UW title and reached the semi-final of the UAU. Thomas was described as: "… one of the most promising young players in Welsh cricket". He gained a first-class degree in mathematics and in his University team were the afore-mentioned rugby star Bryan Richards and future staff cricket club member Ken Walters. [5] The cricketers were UW champions again in 1957 and 1959.

In 1955 the basketball club pleaded for players to join in order to help fulfill friendly and local league fixtures. Later in the decade the club fielded some interesting characters. Howard Mounce, Russell Evans, Brian Wilshire and Peter Davies were part of the team for a match against Bangor in 1958. Mounce sustained a sprained ankle and took no further part in the game while: "Peter Davies was outstanding in scoring thirty points". [6] After graduating, the four players became distinguished academics on the University staff and continued playing and influencing the game by turning out

The 1940s and 50s

for the Swansea Academicals in the local league.

Badminton attracted more members. They won two out of three matches in the UW championship in 1952 and were regarded as a powerful force. Among those representing UW were G Penry and Ian Hart King. The table tennis club entered two teams into the Swansea and District League but withdrew in 1955 due to administrative problems. The popularity of squash was slow to emerge for there was little evidence of the boom of interest in a sport that was to show nationally in the Seventies. Even in the mid-Sixties it was admitted to me by a former student that although he was a regular user of the playing fields, it took him three years to become aware of the location of the courts and that he was sometimes baffled by the appearance from behind the pavilion of: "... exhausted-looking students carrying rackets". The location of the squash courts entrance tucked away at the back of the swimming pool tended to disguise their existence. However, one student who discovered them early in his student days was John Lomax. He entered the University in 1950 following national service, to study engineering. Lomax had never seen a squash court before and took up the game as a beginner. He made rapid progress and in his third year became secretary of the club and his ability on court developed well enough for him to represent and captain the UW team. In recalling his University days, Lomax mentioned purchasing a season ticket for the Mumbles Train on which he travelled for his daily commute to the University. He eventually acquired a motorcycle as a mode of transport. This acquisition, along with his daily attire of blazer and tie – in accordance with the more formal student fashion of the day – no doubt went some way to attract his future wife Diana Jones, who was a secretary in the botany department. Lomax went on to enjoy a successful career in the construction industry and was awarded an OBE for his services to health and safety. [7]

Boxing was revived in 1954-55 after a lapse of several years.

It was well served by John Ford who represented UW. He was an all-round sportsman and acted as chair of CAB. The boxers were crowned UW champions in 1957-58 with Gerry Griffiths as captain. He won a UAU title and boxed for Wales. Novices were encouraged to join the 'blood and bandage sport' and the progress of heavyweight Howard Mounce (previously mentioned retiring from a basketball game) was recognised. The UW championship was held at Swansea in 1959 and enthusiastically supported by student spectators.

New clubs were formed including snooker (1949-50), golf (1952), fencing (1958) and rifle in the same year. Judo was accepted into the CAB fold at the end of the decade by which time the number of student clubs had increased to twenty.

As part of a general societal interest in the outdoors and the natural environment a 'Beacons' club was formed that promoted rambling in the Brecon Beacons and the Black Mountains. In 1952 outings were arranged on alternate Sundays. The numbers interested in cycling increased. They also met on Sundays and a trip was arranged with an overnight stay at a youth hostel in Crickhowell. The possibility of a rowing club emerged following an approach by Mumbles Rowing Club offering tuition for beginners based on a subscription. Aberystwyth, Bangor and Cardiff already had rowing clubs. The lure of Swansea Bay saw a sailing club formed in 1958 and a team was sent to the UW regatta held at Lisvane reservoir in Cardiff. The club only owned one boat (an Enterprise), but negotiated membership with Mumbles Sailing Club.

Intramural sport was given renewed attention when a sports day was organised in 1951. It was regarded as the most successful ever with four records broken and sprinter Lynn Jones winning the men's 100 and 220-yards races. The following year Jones (by now the west Wales sprint champion) repeated his victories and added the 440-yards to become Victor Ludorum. Kathleen Reilly was deservedly crowned Victrix Ludorum. The inter-faculty shield was won by Pure

UNIV. COLL. WALES, SWANSEA.   R.F.C. 1920-21.

BACK ROW :—W. P. REES. S. HUGHES. D. A. SALTER. R. P. PENNINGTON. C. DAVIES. H. E. G. RICHARDS.
M TAHANY. P. W. D. JONES. A. C. JONES.
MIDDLE ROW :—C. POWELL. D. A. EVANS. K. RICHARDS. I. WILLIAMS (*Capt.*) R. A. COUND. T. J. WESTCOTT.
FRONT ROW :—W. FRAYNE. J. H. MORGAN.

The earliest club to represent the University

The Central Athletics Board (CAB) 1926 (founded 1921-22)

UNIVERSITY COLLEGE OF SWANSEA.

INTER - COLLEGIATE WEEK 1925.

Official Programme - 3d.

Inter Coll week programme

Women's hockey at Aberystwyth 1924

Netball at Bangor 1924

Women's hockey 1925

Men's hockey 1920s

Men's football 1925

Men's hockey 1920s

Men's cricket at Pontardawe 1923

Men's rugby 1927 (Watcyn Thomas capt; future Wales capt)

Claude Davey and Idwal Rees (both Wales captains)

March 7th 1927

Dear Sir,

As I have been selected to play for Wales versus Ireland on March 12th, I have two requests to make. First, I ask permission to absent myself from college duties during this time and secondly, I ask that I be excused sitting the Lent terminal examinations which begin on March 17th. My position is this. The Welsh team sails for Ireland on Thursday March 10th. Before this two days will have to be sacrificed in order to attend practices of the Welsh team previous to their sailing for Ireland. I have no definite information as to when the Welsh team will return from Ireland, but in all probability this will be on Sunday March 13th, arriving home on the 14th. This arrangement will not allow me to start work in preparation for the terminal examinations until March 15th. Exams begin for me on the 17th. Assuming that you grant me permission to go to Ireland, the time at my disposal on my return is, in my opinion, too limited to enable me to do anything like examination room work. Hoping that this request will be received favourably.

I am Yours faithfully
Watcyn Thomas

Letter from Watcyn Thomas to the University registrar, 7th March 1927, requesting leave of absence to play for Wales

Opening of the Sports Pavilion at Sketty Lane 1932

Gymnastics club 1933

Gymnastics tableaux 1933

Harriers 1930s

Harriers team 1930s

Cricket 1st XI 1938 (Wyndham Davies capt)

Intra-mural Athletics programme (Sports Day)

UNIVERSITY COLLEGE OF SWANSEA.

SIXTH ANNUAL

ATHLETIC SPORTS

(Under A.A.A. Laws)

TO BE HELD AT

The Playing Fields,

On Wednesday, March 9th, 1938.

Official Programme - One Shilling.

Diary extract, advice on keeping fit 1937

Gwyn Griffiths (long jump),
Vernon Jones (wearing blazer),
Anthony Rees (track athlete).
Sports Day 1938

Hints to "Freshers."

ALWAYS LOOK AT THE NOTICE BOARDS.

Come to the "Freshers'" Social, October 5. "Freshers" free!

Attend Debates and speak at them.

Ask advice from, or make complaints to your S.U.C. representatives, or see the Secretary of S.U.C.

THERE MAY BE A LETTER FOR YOU IN THE PIGEON HOLE. MAKE A DAILY HABIT OF LOOKING THERE.

At the beginning of the Lent Term you become an elector. Make use of your vote in the Annual Elections.

Learn the College Yell and Bloedd y Brifysgol.

Write and sketch for "Dawn," the College magazine which is distributed free to all students.

Get to know about the N.U.S. Buy and read the "New University," 2d. per copy.

Take part in athletics; roll up for practices; make full use of the facilities provided by the Playing Fields and the Pavilion.

If you feel hot and bothered after lectures, go over to the Pavilion, take a run over the common, and end up with a shower bath.

Remember that the upkeep of the Playing Fields costs us £250 per annum. It is a breach of good sense to lounge and smoke in the Common Room when facilities for open air exercise are granted you.

Look out for announcements concerning organized Swedish Drill on the Playing Fields.

Come to dances and socials, attend general meetings.

KINDLY PATRONISE THE ADVERTISERS.

University 1st XV 1936-37. (Haydn Tanner and Willie Davies, sitting next to each on the ground, left to right)

George Edwards (capt 1st XI football, late 1930s-early 1940s), future Wales international

Home Guard unit comprising of students and staff

MEN'S HOCKEY CLUB.

Men's hockey 1942 (note the motley shirts!)

Back row—M. C. Coates, D. C. Rees, D. R. G. Davies, S. G. Young, C. W. Owen, P. Hayes, A. Leaker.
Seated—J. R. Davies, D. Harry, G. Bennett, H. Lloyd, E. J. R. Jones.

Men's rugby 1944 (note the lack of washing powder!)

First post-war rugby XV 1946-47. Vernon Jones and Alun Thomas circled

Rugby 1st XV UW Champions 1948-49. (Vivian Davies capt)

Official programme. Rugby Charity Match 10th May 1947

1st XI cricket. UW Champions 1953-54 (RH Thomas capt)

Bryan Richards 1st XV capt Cambridge, Swansea RFC and Wales

John Gow 1st XI football capt early 1950s. International referee 1960s-70s

Howard Davies (centre) and training partners Lynn Davies (left) and Nick Williams at Sketty Lane. Late 1960s

Cy Knibb receiving the UAU Unicorn Trophy from Sir Denis Howell MP 1965

Athletics meeting at Sketty Lane. Late 1960s

1st XI football 1961-62. (Alan Hopkins capt)

Rowing club ('christening' of new boats with Principal Parry) 1963

Basketball team 1963. (Wayne Stephens capt)

Water polo team 1967-68. (Ted Motley capt)

UNIVERSITY COLLEGE OF SWANSEA WATER POLO TEAM 1966~1967.

J. PALMER   D. ROBINSON   A. GRAHAM-BISHOP   D. ALLMAN   B. STOTTER   T. HUDSON [COACH]

J. FORBES   B. MUNDY   E. MOTLEY [CAPTAIN]   R. HYDE   P. WILLIS

Netball team 1966-67. (Janet Atkinson capt)

COLLEGE 4 BANGOR 0

Pugh & Maggs dominate attack

SWANSEA UNIVERSITY
v
BANGOR UNIVERSITY

U. W. Championship
Wednesday 11th October

Swansea kicked off with a considerable following wind. The opening exchanges were fairly even, play sweeping from end to end with both defences taking time to settle. With 15 minutes gone, Swansea began to get on top and the Bangor team was forced back. However, the visitors occasionally looked dangerous on breakaways and M. Jones was forced to clear off the goal line following a goal-mouth melee. But after 20 minutes Swansea deservedly took the lead. A throw in on the left was followed by a cross from J. Pyrke and Maggs headed a brilliant goal from 15 yards, giving goalkeeper Painter no chance.

The College, now clearly on top, nearly increased their lead

SWANSEA UNIVERSITY
v
SULLY

Sunday 8th Oct.

In an extremely hard fought and even battle the College did well to retain their unbeaten record.

Throughout the first half the play switched evenly from one end to the other, with neither attack being able to make much impression on two solidly organised defences. Of the attacks in the first half, College probably came nearest to scoring with centre forward Vokes causing near panic at times and allowing Pugh more freedom of movement than would normally be allowed. The College back four, Jones, Lees, Rose and Hepworth played well together and with good covering held the Sully attack at bay.

1st XI football 1972. Match report

UAU Football Final programme, 10th March 1970

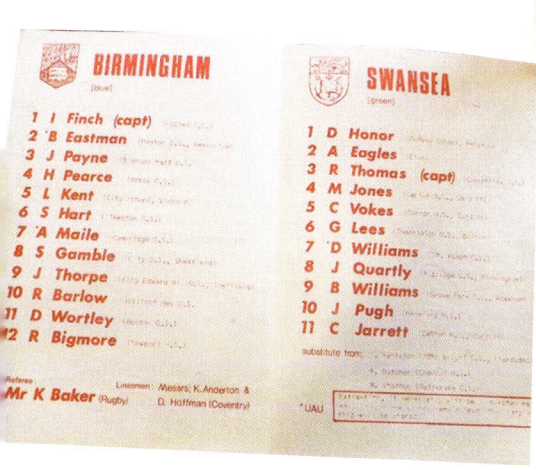

BIRMINGHAM
(blue)

1 I Finch (capt)
2 B Eastman
3 J Payne
4 H Pearce
5 L Kent
6 S Hart
7 A Maile
8 S Gamble
9 J Thorpe
10 R Barlow
11 D Wortley
12 R Bigmore

Referee: Mr K Baker (Rugby)
Linesmen: Messrs. K. Anderton & D. Hoffman (Coventry)

SWANSEA
(green)

1 D Honor
2 A Eagles
3 R Thomas (capt)
4 M Jones
5 C Vokes
6 G Lees
7 D Williams
8 J Quartly
9 B Williams
10 J Pugh
11 C Jarrett

substitute from:

*UAU

UNIVERSITIES ATHLETIC UNION
ASSOCIATION FOOTBALL CHAMPIONSHIP
FINAL
BETWEEN
SWANSEA
AND
BIRMINGHAM
LOCKHEED-LEAMINGTON F.C.
Tuesday 10th March 1970
Kick off 7.30   Programme 6d

Swansea's winning team against Birmingham

Sub-aqua club European endurance record breakers 1973

UCS 1st XV UW CHAMPIONS

SWANSEA 22   ABERYSTWYTH 3   SWANSEA UNIVERSITY 10
                                                         U.W.I.S.T. 3

College became U.W. champions for the first time for seven

Rugby 1st XV win away at Aberystwyth 1972

1966-67. GEOFFREY DALE
1967-69. FRANK SNAPE
1969-71. JOHN FORBES
1971-72. CHRISTOPHER HENSHAW
1972-74. CHRISTOPHER HOWCROFT
1974-75. MICHAEL STEARS
1975-76. PETER STEWART
1976-77. ALLAN HUMPHRIES
1977-78. ANGELA NUNN
1978-79. STEPHANIE LINDSAY
1979-80. BILL FRASER-HARRIS
1980-81. CLIVE JOHNSON
1981-82. DECLAN JORDAN
1982-83. GLENIS WEILDING
1983-84. IAN HOWES
1984-85. RICHARD JARVIS
1985-86. JULIE WILSON
1986-87. KATHARINE GRANT
1987-88. GRAEME GOUDIE
1988-89. MICHAEL LEE
1989-90. JON LEWIS
1990-91. VIV CLEMENT
1991-92. PAUL BENNELL
1992-93. NICK CORRIGAN
1993-94. GETHIN R. JENKINS
1994-95. PHILIP E. DENNIS
1995-96. CELIA McCONNELL
1996-97. ANDREW JOHN
1997-98. PHILIPPA J. DOVE
1998-99. DAVID C. BRINSDEN
1999-00. PETER D. MANNION
2000-01. MARTYN WILLIAMS
2001-02. RICHARD LANCASTER
2002-03. LAWRIE INMAN
2003-04. MICHAEL HARDING
2004-05. BEN TAYLOR
2005-06. BEV BLACKBURN
2006-07. TIMOTHY STICKLEY

Athletic Union Presidents' Board

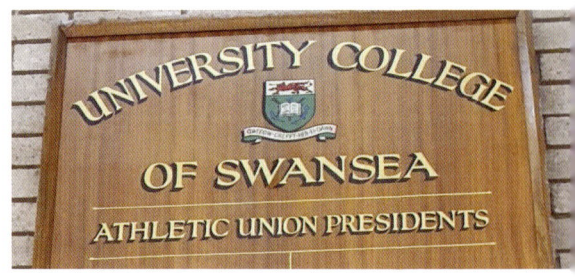

UNIVERSITY COLLEGE OF SWANSEA
ATHLETIC UNION PRESIDENTS

Science. At the close of the Fifties an Inter Departmental Committee (IDC) was formed to organise the popular sports of rugby and football and it was accepted into the CAB.

By the end of the decade much of the hangover from the post-war period had been shaken off and the Fabulous Fifties turned into a time when people were told that: "You've never had it so good". It was to be an era of University expansion and progress in sport.

CHAPTER THREE

The 1960s and 70s: 'swinging and singing'

THE 'SWINGING SIXTIES' was a decade of cultural change. There was large-scale employment and an increase in leisure opportunities. The period enjoyed a revolution in film, music, fashion and television accompanied by greater experience in worldwide travel. James Bond, Beatlemania and the mini skirt caught the imagination of many. A rise in feminism, the hippie movement and a tendency for confrontation and permissiveness pervaded the decade that ended with the celebrated first moon landing in 1969.

On the national sporting scene inspiration came from various sources. Greater television coverage added more professionalism while the Tokyo Olympics (1964) and gold medal winners Lynn Davies and Mary Rand boosted the popularity of athletics. In 1966 England won the football World Cup and closer to home, Glamorgan were County Cricket champions in 1969. Two significant appointments were made in Welsh sport, Ron Pickering to Welsh Athletics and Ray Williams to the WRU. They strengthened the scientific approaches to coaching while the establishment of the Sports Council (1965) by the UK government sought to rationalise the development and administration of sport.

Partly due to the Robbins Report (1963) there was a rise

The 1960s and 70s

in the number of University students. Seven new universities were built in England and ten technological universities were created including the University of Wales Institute of Technology (UWIST). At Swansea student numbers grew from 1,650 to over 3,000. There were building schemes across campus including sports facilities and staffing changes to accompany the growing numbers. [1]

In 1966 Celia Hall joined the staff as an assistant in physical education and recreation. She was the first full-time female appointment to encourage women's sport and had qualified at the Chelsea College of Physical Education. On taking up her Swansea post she remarked: "Let's show the boys that these are our facilities as much as theirs". In the same year Olympic pentathlete and army-trained Tom Hudson replaced Bernard Warden as gymnasium superintendent and instructor in physical recreation. Hudson's wide interests included water polo, squash and fitness training from which many students were to benefit. John Jones (succeeding Hugh Jones) and Don Lewis became head groundsmen at Sketty Lane and Fairwood Playing Fields respectively.

Additional facilities were needed for the growing number of students. Some were built for the long term while others were of a more temporary nature. The newly-acquired Fairwood Estate was completed for sport in 1966. [2] It included a plateau with six football, three rugby pitches and three cricket squares serviced by a pavilion. An indoor rifle range and armoury was added in 1967. It also accommodated lacrosse, had a cross-country course and a fishing lake. At its best the plateau was an exhilarating sight when all nine fields were in use. Yet down the years a constant battle with drainage problems (caused by boulder clay) resulted in many cancellations and frustrated users. Fairwood was at its best when the weather was kindest, and Lewis (followed by Kevin Roberts) toiled diligently to prepare and repair the playing surfaces until his retirement in 1994. He does recall however meeting some prominent football personalities who brought their teams to train at the grounds. These included Swansea City FC managers John Toshack and Harry Gregg. He also met Don Revie of Leeds United and England along with Sir Alf Ramsey, England World Cup winning manager, when they prepared their teams for matches at the Vetch Field.

There was extra indoor facility provision made at Sketty Lane and on the Singleton campus, both of an ad hoc nature. A storage area at the side of the gymnasium was converted to a weight training room (1967) and an old engineering building on campus was adapted as a sports annexe (1969) to provide a hall for basketball, badminton, five-a-side football and other activities. There was also a martial arts area and a boxing ring. These arrangements along with the hiring of local facilities such as the Drill Hall in Richardson Street were to serve students until the opening of the new Sports Centre in 1979. Other outdoor developments occurred at Sketty Lane with the provision of a new cinder athletics track and field events area that was ready for use in 1965. As part of the installation there was a reconfiguration of the rugby, football, hockey and cricket pitches. In 1969 a boathouse and base were provided at Cwm Lliedi Reservoir in Swiss Valley, Llanelli for the needs of the rowing club.

Further significant development affected student sport. Signs were apparent during the previous decade that SRC politics were encroaching upon CAB matters. Discussions and debates arose concerning the desire for sport and its finances to be run by 'sports' people. In 1965 Cy Knibb was elected as chair of CAB. The committed and enthusiastic Knibb transferred his endurance from the running track to his first CAB meeting, for it reportedly lasted six hours. He instigated a CAB annual dinner to encourage a sense of identity and solidarity and implemented changes to formulate an Athletic Union (AU). The AU (regarded as 'Knibb's brainchild') was to receive more independence, its own governance structure and a direct share of the students' amalgamation fee. This was achieved by 1966 when Geoff Dale was elected as the first AU president. Pam Williams was appointed permanent secretary/ treasurer and Dr W T Williams as the staff treasurer. [3]

In light of the above changes how did the sports clubs fare during the Sixties? Early in the decade the rugby club was well served by Keith Crockett (later a successful schools coach), forwards David Balchin, Martin Day, David James and Maesteg RFC player Dilwyn Lloyd. Scrum-half and future airline pilot Lynn Frame scored the first try of the 1961-62 season in a match against Trostre and the club had a budding international in Brian Davies who played for Llanelli, Neath and Wales. His brother Stuart followed him into the University.

At this point, I modestly request some indulgence for a brief personal reminiscence. In 1962-63 a *Western Mail* report on a UW match between Swansea and Bangor at Sketty Lane was headed: "Bangor set to take UW title". The report went on: "... the north Walians held the powerful home side and thanks to some astute play by inside-half Stan Addicott were able to share the honours ... the Swansea pack with wing-forward Stuart Davies outstanding always worried Bangor". [4] The drawn game was enough to put Bangor on the road to securing the title for the first time in thirty-six years. This was my first ever visit to Swansea University and little did I realise then that I would return less than ten years later, having been appointed to the staff in 1971. In those student days I played alongside Stuart Davies and other Swansea players including Huw Jones, Byron Broadstock, Lyn Thomas and Colston Herbert in UW and UAU teams. Davies captained the University club and went on to enjoy a long and successful career as a centre with the All Whites.

A Sixties highlight for the rugby club was a share of the UAU championship in 1964-65 under the captaincy of Glyn Morgan. Following a semi-final replay win over Loughborough, Swansea met Durham at Birmingham to decide the title. In a hard-fought game the result was a draw after extra time. Forwards Phil Hayward, Dai Steele, Dave Winslett, John Evans and future 'medic' Brian Willis stood out during the season alongside backs David James, Eddie Friend and Cyrus Price.

During the decade the University was blessed with a number of good players, teams and captains who later made their mark in Welsh rugby. Albert Parkin (the first Englishman to captain the side), Llanelli centre Mel Smaje, David Pulling and Ian Myhre took turns at leadership. In 1967, during Graham Griffin's tenure, the University defeated Swansea Athletic in a match: "... noted for its disgusting brutality ... filthy weather and even filthier opposition". Strong words from the *Crefft* reporter but thankfully just a blip in cordial relations enjoyed between the two teams down the years. Prominent players included Mike Bassett from Barry, who later in his professional life became Keeper of Geology at the National Museum of Wales. Also, Robert Wood (a great servant to Rhymney RFC) and, before the end of the decade, Robin Barlow, who during his teaching career joined the aforementioned Bryan Richards on the staff at Rugby school. Another was Owen Jones who won a blue at Oxford, became a first-class referee and a headteacher at Amman Valley Comprehensive School. In addition, Hywel Francis, who in his student rugby playing days was positioned on the right wing. While never feeling comfortable being called a 'right-winger', he later enjoyed a political career as Labour MP for Aberavon, a position that placed him (with his Communist leanings) well to the left and far from any association with the right. Francis, a renowned historian, also served the University as professor of adult and continuing education and directed much energy to creating closer ties between the University and Valley communities. In November 1969, politics and rugby clashed violently down the road at St Helen's when anti-apartheid demonstrators (including University students and staff) confronted police and stewards while attempting to disrupt the Swansea RFC match against the touring South African Springboks team.

A strong and regular feature of universities in the Sixties (carried on from the Fifties) was the singing culture that accompanied post-match celebrations amongst rugby clubs and, to a lesser extent other sports clubs too, especially after UW championship games. Swansea teams often gathered in the back room at the Rhyddings Hotel with their opponents of the day. The varied entertainment included drinking games and the singing of a mixture of the 'college medley', bawdy songs, popular ballads and Welsh hymns. Each Welsh college followed suit and had its own favourite pub with a sympathetic landlord and a choirmaster (often a mature student) who brought some discipline and harmony to the songsters. The singing tradition continued into the Seventies and later but seems now to have gone out of fashion, perhaps largely due to revised competition formats and travel arrangements. Other social activities included annual dinners and Easter tours to Cornwall or the northwest of England. In 1968, on one such tour former captain Dai Barry, playing in his last match for the University, scored his first and only try after four years of effort. His daughter Helen was to be a far more prolific scorer for the ladies' basketball team in the early Nineties.

Amongst women students, the hockey club had the largest membership. The club started successfully in 1960-61 encouraged by ten freshers turning up for trials and winning their first match against BP Llandarcy under captain Annette Morgan. During the following years they competed well in WIVAB rallies led by enthusiastic captains, and turned out victors at Birmingham under Fiona MacDonald. Goalkeeper Pam Jordan, "despite her small, slight stature was fearless on the field and a tireless leader off it". [5] During the decade the girls enjoyed tours to Dublin, Cork and Belgium and also twenty-first birthday celebration parties at the Sketty Lane pavilion when the caretaker's wife, Mrs Jones, was 'bribed with bars of chocolate' to gain access. Ann Weekes, captain in 1967 recalls the conviviality of the club: "For most, being involved with hockey was the highlight of our time at Swansea. Training was limited but great effort was put into playing, both on and off the field, possibly more of the latter. Playing alongside the rugby team – literally as the pitches at Sketty Lane were adjacent to one another – resulted in close camaraderie and some even closer relationships between rugby and hockey players". [6]

The "closer relationships" referred to above led to a happy marriage between herself and the aforementioned rugby player Stuart Davies. This is one example of relationships forged through sport. A variety of family connections have been spawned down the years that saw the likes of fathers and sons, mothers and daughters, brothers and sisters and every other form of family link becoming part of the University, often with common sporting connections. Too many to mention, but all contributed to a feeling that Swansea was a special place to study.

The netball club experienced mixed fortunes. In 1963 they earned a deserved, if narrow, victory over a strong Barry Training College team when Ann Webb was captain. However, she stated that in her opinion: "... girls in college adopt an apathetic attitude towards sport and other activities". This comment was made mainly to hide her disappointment at failing to raise a second team of sufficient strength to avoid a heavy defeat against their Barry opponents. Strength in depth had grown sufficiently by 1967-68 for the 2nd VII dilemma seemed to be resolved when the team reached their WIVAB final. The 1st VII were UW champions three times consecutively towards the end of the decade and the club successfully hosted a WIVAB rally in Swansea for the first time. Rhymney girl Janet Atkinson (1968-69) was amongst a line of enthusiastic captains while Gaynor Phillips proved to be an outstanding player and represented WIVAB.

The 1960s and 70s

Along with hockey and netball, the women continued to have their own badminton, squash, fencing and table tennis clubs. Two teams of the latter sport were entered into the local leagues and this experience helped them win the UW championship in 1962-63. Archery gained CAB status in 1964-65 and Margaret Savage led the club at the end of the decade. Winter practice took place in the gymnasium while during the summer shooting was carried out in the open air at Fairwood. Lacrosse made an appearance at Fairwood towards the end of the decade in 1968 when Nest Hughes took on the leadership and Pamela Sutton was captain in 1969-70.

Returning to men's sport, the football club had a memorable decade. Early in the Sixties Alan Hopkins captained the 1st XI and the UW team. He also played for the British Universities in a European tournament in Belgium. Goalkeeper Eric Bowers was also in the UW side. George Evans another club captain, followed his student days by remaining at the University as a member of staff in the French department. In 1966 the club entered the Welsh League and benefited from an early hat-trick from Dave Painter and twenty goals before Christmas from prolific scorer Dave Thomas. There was a promotion to the Premier League followed by a quick relegation.

The 1967-68 season saw unprecedented success when the 1st XI became UAU champions for the first time, beating Newcastle by four goals to two in the final at Leamington. According to UAU officials the team gave: "... a display that ranks them as one of the best post-war sides in the competition". [7] The 1st XI had a clutch of outstanding players including mathematics student Peter Suddaby who went on to Oxford to gain a blue before turning professional and playing in the first division of the Football League for Blackpool. Phil Raybould played for the Wales Amateur XI against Scotland scoring the winning goal and scored the winner too for Swansea Town against Rochdale. Geoff Anthony and Tony Nantcurvis also represented the Wales Amateur XI while six Swansea students were in the UW team that beat the English Universities in 1967. Alongside the above J Clark, K Grant, D Winter, A Eagles, A Turner, D Painter and D Thomas formed the team that won the UAU cup

At the end of the decade the 1st XI won the UAU title again with six freshmen in the side, beating Birmingham in the final under the captaincy of Roger Thomas. Clive Vokes was in the winning side and later served as 1st XI captain. There was promotion too, back to the Welsh League Premiership. Vokes gave much of the credit for the success of the club during his years to 'father figure' and PhD student Mike Dixon who served as team manager. Other notable players during the Sixties included John Baylis who played for Barry Town and later became professor of politics at the University. Also, Geraint Jenkins, a fervent Swans fan who wrote *The History of Swansea City AFC* during his days as professor of Welsh history at Aberystwyth. Goalkeeper Mike Staddon was a competitive and enthusiastic local club cricketer in his post-University days. If luck ever deserted him on the sports field, it was certainly with him on St David's Day in 2006 when he gained public fame by winning £1.3 million on the National Lottery. One further achievement came from Bruce George, another football-loving student of the Sixties. Though not a playing member of the football club, he was a qualified and active referee. George was elected Labour MP for Walsall South in 1974. His enthusiasm for sport led him to become founder, goalkeeper and captain of the House of Commons football team known as the Westminster Warblers – another example of sport mixing with politics. [8]

The athletics club was also blessed with some top-class talent. All club fixtures were away from home until the new track opened. In 1963-64 there were indoor meets at RAF Cosford and St Athan, followed by a successful tour to Germany. In 1965 the club won the UAU Unicorn Trophy that was presented to Cy Knibb by Denis Howell, Minister for Sport. Some outstanding athletes made good use of the new track facilities that opened in 1965, including Olympic gold medallist Lynn Davies and his coach Ron Pickering. They travelled frequently from Cardiff and inspired the students. The athletics club captain Howard Davies became a Commonwealth Games 400m runner and the University's first Olympian in Mexico City in 1968. He stated that: "I still have a very strong affection for Swansea... the University was the place where my athletics career started and has proved to be very kind to me over many years." Chemistry student and shot putter Alan Carter was a Great Britain (GB) athlete, UAU champion and World Student Games competitor. Triple jumper Nigel Greene represented Wales and the Amateur Athletics Association (AAAs) and following graduation, moved to Oxford to gain his blue. Pauline Hardingham, Christine Thomas, Christine Tringham and Hilary Knock performed well in women's teams while Janet Jones was captain in 1969-70.

The University harriers were always competitive with Nog Williams, Neil Kemp, Bob Hazlewood, Mike Draffin, Rod Totterell and David Jones to the fore. On leaving University, Jones was to give dedicated service to Swansea harriers over a long period of time. Training sessions at Merthyr Mawr sand dunes and events such as the West Glamorgan League races at Fairwood, Hyde Park Relays, Gower Eleven and the *Evening Post* Trophy offered the athletes and harriers opportunities to show their form. The Hyde Park race was always enjoyable but in the words of team captain Draffin there was usually "glamour but no glory".

Growing enthusiasm in the basketball club continued from the Fifties. Early in the decade under the captaincy of Welsh international Wayne Stephens, the club went on a winning run of twelve matches. During his post-University RAF career, Stephens became officer in charge of basketball at St Athan. At Swansea he was well supported by fellow Welsh internationals and UAU players David Davies, Bob Hancock and Nigel Greene, the latter becoming a 'double international' in association with athletics. The club fielded two teams in the Swansea and District League. They were winners in the Three Counties Tournament and the West Wales Challenge Shield competition. An absorbing match in the Swansea and District League saw the students come up against Swansea Academicals, the staff team referred to in the previous chapter. The match ended in a win for the students by 84-83 after extra time. The close result indicates the intensity of the 'battle' with no quarter asked or given by either side, but the eventual honour going to the 'young blood'. The students were regular winners of the UW championships and came third in the UAU finals in 1968. From the mid-Sixties the club featured in the National Basketball League involving English clubs and some matches were played at the Drill Hall in Richardson Street.

Interest in table tennis increased and there was a run of success when the men won six UW championships and reached two UAU finals before losing to Birmingham on both occasions. Eddie Groves took a turn as captain but the outstanding player from 1962-65, who led Swansea and UW teams, was Paul Gilbertson. In the mid-Sixties there were three men's and two women's teams competing in the district leagues. Other indoor sports clubs with smaller numbers of competitors continued to be active. The rifle club was based at Llandarcy until the Fairwood range was ready. The snooker club entered the local league for the first time in 1963-64 under the guidance of Mal Davies and fresher Roy Leach from Aberdare, came into prominence when winning the club championship against John Charlston in "the best final for three years".

Volleyball, a new indoor sport was introduced in1966-67. Student Owen Brown, a Trinidadian international player, gathered enough support to form a team. Aided by members of the Townhill club, the students practised enthusiastically. An inaugural match was arranged against Bristol at the Drill Hall and Swansea turned out victors.

The badminton club bemoaned the lack of facilities when struggling to accommodate a growing membership This did not deter their enthusiasm and by 1966-67 two practices a week were being held at the Drill Hall. The UW championship was won on three occasions and in 1964-65 the Swansea team were chosen en-bloc to represent UW in the BUSF tournament. Mohammed Anis was an outstanding captain who represented the UAU and his successor R B Greenwood helped maintain the club's standards. Men's squash also grew in popularity early in the decade. The team included Norman Ratcliffe, who later became a professor at the University and a stalwart over many years for the Academicals squash team. There was a successful period up until 1968-69 during which time Pindi Mangat, Jon Swift, Nigel Orrett and Steve Gebbett amongst others, represented UW. In the summer racket sport, men's tennis won two UW championships during the mid-Sixties.

The 1st XI hockey team were UW champions at the beginning and end of the decade. The club enjoyed two tours to Dublin and involved themselves in St Patrick's Day celebrations and visits to the Guinness brewery. Such activities no doubt affected their match results, but Ian Towler and Dafydd Herman-Smith were steadying influences within the club. The golf club succeeded in winning the UW championship in 1967-68 and used Langland Bay GC for matches and practice. Don Nuttall took over the captaincy the following season. Cricket was often affected by examinations, the short summer term and the vagaries of the weather, but a four-match tour to the Oxford area was eventful and successful despite being rain affected. Tanganyika (now Zanzibar) off-spinner Raj Veghella was selected for the UAU. The team were UW champions in 1967 and Tudor Thomas was elected captain for the following year, enabling him to transfer his athleticism from rugby to the cricket field. Inspiration for the University batsmen came in August 1968 when cricket history was made at St Helen's. West Indian star Garfield Sobers hit a record six sixes in an over off the bowling of Malcolm Nash in a county match between Glamorgan and Nottinghamshire.

Interest in the martial arts grew and boxing maintained support. In 1963 two influential figures in British judo were involved in a Festival of Sport at the Brangwyn Hall. Charles Palmer (chair of the British Judo Association, and later chair of the British Olympic Association) with Swansea Olympian Alan Petherbridge (principal of Swansea Judo Club) took the opportunity to promote the sport. Palmer stated that: "I would like to see the University students and the LEA work with Alan Petherbridge to introduce judo to a wide mass of people". [9] Judo was a growing sport nationally and the plea was acted upon. In 1967-68 PhD student, AU president and judo club captain Frank Snape brought his influence to bear for the purchase of a new tatami mat to cater for the needs of the club's sixty student players. A series of classes was held in aikido towards the end of the decade to introduce that sport, while the pugilists from the boxing club entered annual universities championships in Dublin, Liverpool and Bracknell. Tudor Morgan, Peter Rich and Rick Snell earned gold medals from their action in the ring.

Away from the holding and throwing on the judo mat and the blood and sweat of the boxing ring, the swimming pool offered a more tranquil environment. However, competition amongst swimmers and water polo players was no less serious and committed. The swimming club provided twelve representatives for the UW team in 1960 yet it was the water polo club that gained most of the honours during the decade. From the mid-Sixties the club dominated the annual UW tournaments. Peter Strawbridge captained the team in 1963-64 and in the following year Pete Willis, Dave Allman, John Walters and Geoff Haden were regular performers. Walters was chosen for the British Universities. Haden represented UW in swimming and tennis and still found the energy to play 1st XI hockey. He also acted as the founding student treasurer of the newly-formed AU. In his later life he devoted much time and commitment to promoting the memory and works of Dylan Thomas in the Swansea area and beyond. Yorkshireman Ted Motley arrived at the University as a mature student in 1966. Already an experienced GB international he captained the University club, UW, UAU and represented BUSF. Motley was named AU Sportsman of the Year in 1967. He had good support from the likes of Barry Stotter, Brent 'Pancho' Mundy, the six-feet seven-inches tall goalkeeper Graham Bishop, Peter Ripley and others. Swansea reached the UAU final in 1968-69 when they lost to Loughborough in a closely-fought match.

The University is blessed with an outstanding natural environment and students were not slow to follow the growing national interest in the outdoors. 'Adventure' activities were expensive in relation to equipment, storage, maintenance and transport but their popularity was growing. The sailing club purchased six new boats in 1961-62 courtesy of the University, releasing monies from its Welsh Church Acts Fund. The club was able to host the UW championship for the first time at Mumbles in 1964-65. The day's activity was followed by a dinner-dance at the Osborne Hotel where Professor Victor Morgan, the club's commodore, entertained those present with a welcome speech. By 1960 interest in rowing had been intermittent due to a lack of equipment. The Mumbles Rowing Club were always helpful and the CAB had subsidised entry fees for competition. However, in 1963-64 the students' rowing club acquired two new boats and they were named *Elizabeth* and *Katherine* after Principal J H Parry's daughters. The 'launching' was carried out by the principal who reportedly used a large tankard of beer to ritually 'wet' the bows of the boats. [10]

In 1963 a mountaineering club was formed and equipped with ropes, slings and tents. During the following year, Dr Alan Osborne of the zoology department pioneered the founding of sub-aqua activity after delivering an eight-session course on underwater swimming at the University pool. By the end of the decade there was enough interest shown to form a club. Pony trekking and riding began at Pennard in 1967 with Sue Hicks and Sue Hall harnessing support for the activity.

Surfing was gaining international interest in the Sixties and the Gower bays proved to be a great attraction for the activity. The local Gower Surfing Club welcomed students, but they formed their own club in 1967-68 when Dave Shillabeer acquired three new boards for the use of members.

The sky was an attraction for students interested in gliding and towards the end of the decade an application for the formation of a club was granted by the AU on condition of the serving of a successful probationary period. However, the lengthy journey to the gliding base at Withybush Airfield in Haverfordwest was off-putting for members who were not fully committed.

For those who did not want to show an obligation to club sports, a varied intramural programme of activities was available. In 1964-65 the Mid Week League (MWL) replaced the IDL and, by the end of the decade, nineteen football teams were participating, making good use of Fairwood when conditions allowed. With so many teams, there was an appeal in *Crefft* for volunteer referees to officiate the matches. Remuneration was offered at the rate of 7/6 (seven shillings and sixpence in 'old money') per game. There were seventeen teams in a rugby sevens competition at Sketty Lane in 1968 when the metallurgy department beat Lewis Jones Hall in the final.

In 1963 the University swimming championships were held at the pool with events for 'champions and novices'. Hugh Scurlock from the rugby club won the novice race. In the relays the civil engineering society came first in the men's event while the biology department won the ladies. The winning teams were respectively presented with the Peterson Cup and the Peterson Shield, both generously donated by

The 1960s and 70s

enthusiastic swimmer and mathematics lecturer Dr Gordon Peterson. Peterson later in his career took up a post at the University of Canterbury in Christchurch, New Zealand.

The Annual Sports Day held in 1964 included thirteen athletics events for men and eight for women. Not unexpectedly the aforementioned Howard Davies, Alan Carter and Nigel Greene took the honours. The following year, when 'christening' the new track, a full programme was arranged and eight records broken. Ironically, the new facilities brought reluctance on the part of many to take part, due to a feeling of specialisation in the sport. This led to the demise of the annual sports day. The harriers had their own University cross-country championship over a six-and-a-half mile course at Fairwood and Bob Hazlewood was a winner in 1967.

By the end of the decade there was a growing interest in coaching and refereeing courses. Governing bodies of sport were appointing national coaches and organisations like the CCPR were arranging courses for students to gain elementary qualifications in sports of their choice that they could use in schools, clubs and vacation work. These courses were to blossom during the next decade.

Accompanying the positive changes and the enthusiastic take-up of opportunities, periodic and undesirable lapses in acceptable behaviour arose. "There were more and more complaints about college teams ... A drinking culture was blamed and over doing it ... especially on away trips." [11] This type of conduct was to raise its head from time to time in the future to sully the positive experiences enjoyed by the majority of sports men and women. However, the first half-century of student sport was undoubtedly memorable with increased facilities, staffing and the range of sports clubs growing from less than ten in the 1920s to almost forty. The next decade was to bring further changes and challenges.

The 1970s

The Seventies turned into desperate years politically and economically. Financial concerns including high inflation and cuts led to strikes and a three-day working week. Personalities like Margaret Thatcher, Arthur Scargill and David Bowie, in their different ways, captured the complicated, contrary spirit of the decade.

In a lighter cultural vein, the period enjoyed a variety of popular musical offerings like heavy metal, disco, Abba and country and western. TV sitcoms including 'Fawlty Towers', 'Dad's Army', 'Porridge' and films like 'The Godfather', 'Jaws' and 'Rocky' attracted large numbers of viewers. Fashions such as flared trousers, hotpants, platform shoes, moustaches, sideburns, and Mohawk hairstyles were to filter through society onto University campuses.

National influences impacted upon University sport and recreation including a fresh regard for the values of health and physical activity with a boom of interest in aerobics and squash. The Women's Liberation Movement, Title IX of the Educational Amendments Act (1972) in the USA and the Sex Discrimination Act (1975) in the UK brought greater awareness, equal rights policies for women and a more balanced sharing of facilities and finance. A combination of factors reshaped gender roles and relations. There was an increased number of women graduates. The impact of the pill and labour-saving devices in the household gave working women more leisure time to benefit from a plethora of multi-purpose sports centres built in the Sixties and Seventies. These effects were seen on University campuses.

The success of the Welsh rugby team with a clutch of outstanding players like Gareth Edwards, Gerald Davies and Mervyn Davies, coupled with the adoption of a squad and coaching system, attracted a wide following within a strong rugby culture. The emergence of the singer and entertainer Max Boyce brought colour, humour and a renewed national

The 1960s and 70s

consciousness. Boyce's songs like 'Hymns and Arias' have remained a staple Welsh rugby supporters' refrain to this day and have been adopted by other sports. In the early Seventies the University staff were treated to his entertainment at their then annual dinner-dance. Complete with his red and white hat, scarf, mackintosh and six-feet tall imitation leek, he performed in the spirit that made him a popular public figure.

Following discussions during the previous decade, the Sports Council for Wales (SCW) was established in 1972 indicating the government's intention to become formally and strategically involved in sport. Alumnus George Edwards, previously mentioned for his football fame, was invited to join its first board. Dr Huw Jones, former chief executive of the SCW, in paying tribute to Edwards, remarked that: "... on retirement he was dedicated to serving Welsh sport and played a leading role in its strategic thinking at a time that was crucial for the development of sport". [1] He was the earliest of a number of Swansea alumni to serve the Sports Council either in a voluntary or professional capacity in future years. Amongst these were Professors David Herbert and John Baylis along with former Wales rugby captain Paul Thorburn. Others will be referred to in due course.

The economic and political mood of the country was also reflected in the universities. They suffered from economies imposed by the government and students were not slow to protest nationally and locally. University sport was affected from the weekend closure of facilities to save fuel and overtime payments and the withdrawal of sponsorships. Some appointments were frozen, retiring staff not replaced and annual grants cut. At Swansea student numbers had increased to approximately 3,500 by 1971. Sport perhaps suffered less than elsewhere for planning went ahead for a new sports hall that was built towards the end of the decade.

In 1971 staffing changes occurred at Sketty Lane. Both Tom

Hudson and Celia Hall moved on from their positions. I was appointed assistant to Vernon Jones, the lecturer in charge of physical education and recreation. After graduation from Bangor, I had gained a specialist diploma in physical education and a PGCE at Loughborough before teaching in schools in Essex and Merthyr Tydfil. At the same time, Roberta Adams took up a similar post before moving to Liverpool University in 1977. Gwyneth John (later Diment) was appointed in her place. She was a graduate of Anstey College of Physical Education and had teaching experience in Staffordshire. It was to be the start of a long and successful career for her at the University.

During the Seventies there were significant changes in the leadership of the AU. In 1971-72 Chris Henshaw, former table tennis captain, became the first sabbatical president. Due to increased student activities an annual stipend was introduced to allow the president's post to become full-time. Chris 'Jumbo' Howcroft followed Henshaw for a two-year stint. Howcroft was an imposing figure: "... standing six feet six inches tall and weighing twenty-one stones". He was also a key man in the rugby scrum and following a trimming down of his figure, went on to play for London Welsh RFC and the Wales B team. In 1977-78 netball captain Angela Nunn became the first woman president. The fencing club's Stephanie Lindsay was next in post, indicating the fact that women students were readily coming forward to provide a voice for University sport.

How did the AU clubs fare during the Seventies? The rugby club welcomed voluntary assistance from staff members. Professor Bryn Gravenor took on the role of president, Dr David Treharne (chairman), Roger Elias (secretary), Professor David Herbert (fixture secretary) and myself as coach in an effort to preserve some continuity. In 1971 the 1st XV played a WRU Cup match against Llanelli at Sketty Lane. A report on the match stated that: "Gallant tackling was a highlight

The 1960s and 70s

of the student effort but the pace and power of the more experienced Llanelli side fielding three Welsh internationals and one British Lion proved too much ... the large crowd was most appreciative of a thoroughly entertaining game." [2] It was a fine effort from the students against a side that in the following year was to defeat the New Zealand All Blacks at Stradey Park.

In 1972-73 the 1st XV won the UW championship and proceeded to reach the UAU final for the first time in seven years. The road to Twickenham (or Twickers, as described by Max Boyce) opened up for the UAU final was now established annually at that prestigious venue. A strong Loughborough team that included future internationals Fran Cotton, Lewis Dick and Clive Rees were too good for Swansea on the day despite the cajoling of captain Alan Thomas. Two years later Swansea were at Twickenham again for an all-Welsh UAU final against UWIST. Swansea led in the match until the closing minutes when Gareth Davies (future British Lion, Wales international and WRU chairman) dropped a goal for his team following an earlier penalty, to snatch victory from Byron Light's Swansea side by 6-4. Overall it was a decent day for University rugby as all three teams (1sts, 2nds and 3rds) played in their respective finals.

Further honours were gained by Swansea players as Byron Light, Ken Hopkins and Chris Dew went on to Oxford to earn their blues. Chris Lee, Byron Light, Alan Rees, David Protheroe, Gwynfor Higgins and Roy Lewis represented the British Universities and played regular first-class rugby. Three others, Phil May, Gwyn Evans and Mark Wyatt, were future Welsh internationals. Phil May gave outstanding service to Llanelli RFC. Evans played for Maesteg and the British Lions. Wyatt captained both the University 1st XV and the British Universities XV. He also played for the Barbarians and his place-kicking prowess led to him becoming the all-time record scorer for Swansea RFC by accumulating 2,734 points. On retiring from the game, Wyatt exchanged the kicking tee for the golf tee and enjoyed committed service to the Wales Golf Union and membership of the R&A. Alongside these a host of other good players and captains formed the base for successful University teams. These included second row forward Andy Marriott who later taught at Monmouth and Bryanston schools where he coached many talented young players, some of whom he guided to Swansea to boost the University side.

The football club began the Seventies as UAU champions and were also in the Premier Division of the Welsh League. The 1st XI played against some seasoned former professionals and internationals who were in the twilight of their careers, such as Ivor Allchurch. The former Swans, Newcastle and Wales legend on one occasion mesmerised the students with his skills while turning out for Haverfordwest at Sketty Lane. The University club won five consecutive UW championships and reached three UAU semi-finals. They were UAU finalists against Loughborough in 1974-75 but lost narrowly by 1-0 under captain Colin Carr. Steve Kay, John Pyrke, Tim Gill, Larry Cattle, Darryl Sherriff, Andy Fletcher and Dave Rose were amongst those who gave sterling service to the club. Rose was elected Player of the Year and his post-University career saw him appointed to the headship of Maesydderwen Comprehensive School. However, during the decade the club suffered two relegations in the Welsh League finding themselves in Division Two in 1978.

The men's hockey 1st XI enjoyed winning two UW championships in 1971 and 1974 proceeding to the UAU semi-finals on both occasions. The club also reached two Welsh League cup finals but lost both to Cardiff and Newport. The six-feet eight-inches tall John Sayce was an impenetrable goalkeeper. During his post-University days and in retirement he swapped a hockey stick for a bicycle and concerned himself with the well-being of Swansea people by taking on the role of chairman of the Swansea Bay cycle group Wheelrights.

He helped to secure improved cycle routes by supporting the channeling of grants from the government and the local council into linking outlying areas of the city. Allan Humphris was a dedicated hockey captain, a 1st XI cricketer and also served a term as AU president. PhD student Humphris showed the more sentimental and romantic side of his character while in his AU post when he organised a well-supported St Valentine's Day Dinner and Dance at the Top Rank Suite. Peter Martineau, Balder Singh, Ian Muir, Wales U23 international Ian Towler, Gary Cope and Dafydd Herman-Smith were amongst the stalwarts of the club. Following graduation Cope took his hockey skills further afield when he enjoyed a successful time as a head teacher at a school in Argentina. Herman-Smith also caught the travel bug and taught hockey at a secondary school on the idyllic island of Bermuda.

The cricket club's Ian Crawford was selected for the UAU and the MCC in 1978 while at the end of the decade Ian Humphreys took on the role of captain with Dave Clarke as his deputy.

The harriers were regular participants in the annual Gower Eleven and Hyde Park Relays events. The Gower Eleven road race was a popular event that started and finished at Sketty Lane while covering the areas of Bishopston, Caswell, Newton and Oystermouth. The Hyde Park Relays was also a stamina-sapping competition that attracted ninety-four teams during the early Seventies. In the same period the athletics team won a UW indoor meeting at RAF St Athan and the *Evening Post* Trophy against Swansea Harriers AC. Janet Jones, Derek Vaughan, Cliff Vincent, Roger Sampson, Owen Bevan and Tony Gaughan were amongst the staunch members of the University club. Cefn Cribbwr's Adrian Thomas (1970-73) was a GB junior sprinter and a Wales schoolboy international rugby player. After graduation and on retirement from competition, he gave outstanding service to Welsh athletics as a highly respected coach. His commitment saw him manage

71

and coach Wales and GB teams at Commonwealth, European, World and Olympic games.

In the indoor sports John Davies and M Butterfield represented the UAU in badminton and Martin Porter captained the UW squash team. Early in the decade Chris Henshaw and K K Leung guided the table tennis team to the UW championship. The club was also inspired when spectating the appearance of British champion Chester Barnes and English international Trevor Taylor, in a tournament at the Afan Lido, Aberavon. Fencer Mike Styles represented the UAU while fellow clubman and AU president Peter Stewart was awarded full colours in 1976. Basketball players Stuart Culliford, Ray Brierley, Peter Godfrey and Tom Wood were amongst those selected for UW.

During the Seventies women's sports had a strong presence with individuals and teams shining through. Gaynor Phillips (netball), Sue Guneraseka (table tennis), and Maureen Clark (hockey) all represented WIVAB. In 1971 the table tennis club were UW champions and WIVAB finalists. The riding club won the UW championship in 1973 under the captaincy of Val Brown. The competition included dressage, show jumping and cross-country. In the same year the hockey 1st XI had five players in the UW team including Viv Jones and Nicola Hamer. Sue Cousin and Jane Chidgey helped the badminton club win the UW title in 1976-77 and success came the way of the netball club in the following year when the 1st and 2nd teams won UW with Angela Nunn a stand-out player during her time.

There was plenty of interest in boxing and the martial arts. In 1971 the British and Irish Universities and Hospitals Boxing Championships were held in Swansea and vociferously supported by the local crowd. The home team failed to win a medal but there was some redemption in the following year when Peter Rich won the UAU welterweight title. Judo flourished under captain Richard Williams and coach Terry

Bennett. Williams, from Abercynon, later enjoyed a successful business career while living in Silicon Valley, California, and he became a sponsor of the University club. In 1978 the club team were chosen en bloc to represent UW at the BUSF championships at Crystal Palace. By 1978-79 karate was well established and met two evenings a week at the sports annexe on the Singleton campus. Martin Lewis promoted the attractions of the sport in a *Crefft* article which no doubt helped to gain enough support to send three teams to the students' national championships. [3]

Although the opening hours of the swimming pool had been extended to Saturday and Sunday afternoons, competitive swimming and water polo did not reach the heights of the previous decade. However, in lifesaving David Hughes, Stuart Sherman and Andy Muirhead were amongst those who gained full colours. Both Hughes and Sherman represented Wales in the sport while the latter also competed for Great Britain and, following graduation, lived in Australia where he had ample opportunity to develop his skills on that country's popular beaches. Hughes's chemistry studies took him from Swansea to Aberystwyth for a PGCE and on to Cardiff Medical School to qualify as a doctor. Alongside his academic work he also had the distinction of representing each institution in rugby and water polo.

Outdoor activities continued to grow in popularity. There was mountaineering, rock climbing and walking in the Gower, Pembrokeshire, Snowdonia and the Peak District. The sailing club maintained a good membership and hosted the UW championships at Mumbles in 1971. During the following years Ian Carpenter, Richard Harvey, Alan Butchart and Ken Sleeman were amongst the regular participants. Rowing was revitalised with the opening of the boathouse at Cwm Lliedi reservoir but its remoteness from the University had its drawbacks. The canoe club had regular training in slalom and 'Eskimo rolls' at the pool and also organised weekend trips to the Gower coast, and the rivers Usk and Wye. There was fluctuating interest in orienteering although Brian Bullen represented GB in Sweden in 1970 and A P Barnes assisted in forming the Welsh Orienteering Association.

New outdoor activities included sub-aqua, hang gliding and skiing. In 1970 John Smart became diving officer for the sub-aqua club and there were lectures, pool training and visits to the Royal Navy base at Gosport for films and demonstrations. There was also a successful dive by club members off the Pembrokeshire coast. Students were not slow in taking up challenges and in 1973 Pete Etherington-Smith, with the help of Mike Chew, Steve Hodge and Mike Holland, broke the European underwater endurance record at the University pool setting a new time of thirty-three hours and seven minutes. The record-breaking event had full medical supervision and support and was a credit to the enthusiasm and organisation of a relatively new club.

The newly-formed hang gliding club was also up for a challenge and a place in the record books. The club was founded in 1974-75 and acquired a glider in the following year. It soon boasted nearly 100 members and a thorough training scheme of lectures, demonstrations and two-man control techniques was put into place. In an effort to emulate the sub-aqua club's record-breaking success at the pool, training officer Kevin Jordan 'took to the sky' and broke the GB and European endurance record, raising it to twelve hours and fifteen minutes. Popular venues for the activity were the Rhossili and Crickhowell areas.

The ski club was founded in 1970 and contented itself with visits to the Cardiff Dry Ski Slope and organised trips to Aviemore, Austria and Italy. Efforts to stage a realistic event closer to home were thwarted when the first planned UW competition in Snowdonia was cancelled for: "... the only patch of snow large enough was a two-and-a-half-hour walk from the car park!" [4] Wales has never been renowned for its 'snow fields'.

Again, for those not wishing to travel, taste adventure or attempt to break records, intramural sport offered other choices. During the decade eight teams competed in Mid Week League rugby and the Geography Society won both the league and cup competitions. Twenty teams took part in football with the Pseuds and Gilbertson topping their respective divisions. There were fifteen teams of three players per side for a table tennis competition and six teams in a lunchtime basketball league. UW captain Martin Porter was an intramural squash tournament winner. During the summer term cricket matches took place at Fairwood on a challenge basis with departments and societies regularly taking advantage of any balmy evenings to set up stumps.

For individuals wishing to take up a new activity, voluntary instructional classes were available in swimming, lifesaving, racket sports, trampoline, keep fit and roller-skating.

In 1976 there was a thoughtful article written by the *Crefft* sports editor, student Robert Anderson, on the need to develop facilities, increase participation and promote a 'sport for all' policy. He also claimed that there had been a fall-off in sports reporting, for although physical activity was in good swing little mention was being made of sports results in *Crefft*. [5]

By the end of the Seventies many would have been pleased to know that the University had plans to develop sport at Sketty Lane, for the next decade was to open with new structures in place to take sport forward. The first sixty years of the University's existence had been notable, but the remainder of the century was to be even more significant for sports development.

CHAPTER FOUR

The 1980s and 90s: a leap forward, partnerships and progress

Eighties Britain was a controversial decade. Margaret Thatcher served as the first female prime minister and government policies promoted an aggressive privatisation of public sector companies, reflecting a deep shift away from a collective public ethos to an individual, private one. We saw the advent of the 'yuppie' and the 'material girl', high street brand names and designer labels. A club culture developed. Also, there were changing attitudes towards diversity, multiculturalism and worldwide issues such as Aids and Children in Need.

Thatcherism had a sobering effect upon universities. They were targeted for retrenchment and the financial concerns of the Seventies continued. Swansea was obliged to take action with staff reductions, early retirement schemes, recruitment of more overseas students, the reorganisation of departments and income generation from marketable facilities. [1] Despite bearing some of the economic pain, sport gained momentum with the opening of the new Sports Centre at Sketty Lane to which we will return.

During the decade stand-out features in international sport

included the first Olympic boycotts at Moscow (1980) and Los Angeles (1984) and the issue of performance enhancing drugs. Notwithstanding, athletes like Seb Coe, Steve Ovett, Daley Thompson and Wales's Steve Jones and Kirsty Wade were outstanding and successful performers.

Other relevant sporting features of the Eighties included the creation of the Women's Sports Foundation (1984) to increase awareness of women's sport. In 1987 the first Wales women's rugby team was fielded in an international match against England with four Swansea University players included. In the same year the first men's Rugby World Cup was organised and Swansea alumnus Paul Thorburn kicked the winning points for Wales against Australia to secure the bronze medal. Locally, Swansea City FC was promoted to the First Division of the Football League and Swansea RFC had its most successful era since WW1 with myself privileged to act as coach.

Changing attitudes resulted in more diversification in sport. This was apparent in schools where the Education Act of 1986 affected teachers' contracts causing strike action that in turn led to a crisis in PE. Concerns were expressed over the sale of school playing fields. There were debates in the tabloids and on TV (that ran into the following decade) over issues such as the values of team games, the place of competition and elite sport. Health related exercise (HRE) became the mantra for many PE and sports professionals with an increasing interest in diet, aerobics, visits to the gym, yoga and dance. [2] There was a corresponding boost in leisure wear for, as exercise became fashionable, sports clothing such as joggers, leg warmers, leotards, branded football shirts and sports shoes were purchased for gym use and also general wear around University campuses. The greater diversity in sport was illustrated in Wales with the opening of the National Watersports Centre at Plas Menai, Snowdonia, in 1983. By the end of the decade there were eighty-seven sports bodies promoting different activities. Curiously more girls and women became involved in hitherto traditional men's sports such as football and rugby and later films such as 'Bend it like Beckham' and 'Gregory's Girl' fed the interest. These changes, issues and debates affected students, but the University was to be well prepared to meet any challenges.

On the retirement of Vernon Jones who had been in post since 1938, a new staffing structure was put in place with the establishment of a directorate for sport and physical recreation. In 1980 I was appointed director with John Palmer (later, on his retirement, replaced by Paul Hickson) and Gwyneth Diment as assistant directors. Alongside, was an initial group of 'front-of-house' support staff that included Norma Ellis, Bernard Kift, Ken French, Malcolm Jackson and Julie Anderson to help develop the new Sports Centre that was officially opened in 1981. Lord Hunt, leader of the 1953 Conquest of Everest team, Principal Steele, Judge Rowe Harding and Professor Ieuan Williams conducted the ceremonials. Local sports people invited to attend included Wales international football star and Swans manager John Toshack along with All Whites and Wales rugby internationals, David Richards and Roger Blyth. The latter was later to become an honorary fellow of the University. Harold Oakes, director of the Sports Council for Wales was also in attendance. The Percy Thomas Partnership, with Brian Chambers as the lead architect, designed the new centre. Despite the stringent financial policies of the time, funding to the sum of approximately £500,000 was largely drawn from the University's Development Appeal Fund and the Welsh Church Acts Fund.

The main features of the new facilities were the multi-purpose sports hall, indoor climbing wall, three additional squash courts, weight training room, changing areas and a suite of offices all linked up to the existing swimming pool. The new structures provided an enhanced administrative and practical base to take University sport forward.

A further positive step in support for sport came with the introduction of the Sporting and Cultural Scholarships Scheme in 1985, the first of its kind in Wales. Professor Howard Purnell chaired the inaugural scholarships committee. The aim of the scheme was to provide outstanding sportsmen and women with guidance, coaching, expenses, and lifestyle management in order to fulfill their academic and sporting talents. There would also be a boost for sports clubs, University sport in general and student recruitment. In addition bursaries were also made available for suitable applicants who did not reach scholarship standard. Awards were also available for musicians, artists etc.

David Evans, David Bryant, Duncan Rolley and Steve James were the four original scholars. The former two later represented Wales at rugby, Rolley swam for England and GB while Lydney born James played cricket for Glamorgan and England, thus indicating the standards set by the early scholars. Progress on the development of the scheme and additional sources of similar support will be discussed as we proceed but due to the large number of awards granted down the years it will not be possible to name every recipient.

While support was forthcoming for the 'elite' end of sport, the cold wind of financial restriction was hitting the University and a 'pay to play' policy was introduced for sports participation. In 1981-82 charges were made for Sports Centre activities and although not to everyone's liking, Declan Jordan, president of the AU, attempted to pacify students by stating that: "… the charges were only a token amount in these times of cutbacks". The AU itself introduced a Sports Participation Fee (SPF) amongst its club players in 1985-86 due to "an impending cash crisis in the AU". There was controversy with the Students' Union (SU) over this but three presidents, Glenis Weilding, Julie Wilson and Katharine Grant (carrying on from the female leadership shown in the previous decade), helped to ride the storm. [3] At the end of the decade permanent secretary/treasurer Pam Williams, who had given sterling service since the inception of the AU, retired and was followed by Veronica Short.

The AU was also concerned about a fall-off in constructive sports reporting in the student newspaper. *Crefft* was replaced by *Double Take* in 1980. In October 1985 'the twin voices of College sport', John Jarrow and Nick Spencer (*Double Take* sports editors), called for improved sports reporting. It was felt that reports of club matches deserved better than: "... the in-jokes and coded accounts of extra sporting prowess in alcohol consumption and sexual activity which had previously tended to be the case". There was a call to: "... respect the achievements and points of interest within various clubs". This is not to say that many stories (although not directly concentrating on the matches) were without their humour. For example, the occasion when a group of rugby players were left on the streets of Cardiff in the early hours of the morning in freezing conditions, due to missing the team bus back to Swansea after too much celebrating. On appearing to become a potential nuisance, they were taken 'into care' by two patrolling policemen and given a warm cell, with the door left open overnight, at the local police station. At breakfast time, to the relief of the students, the duty sergeant made them a cup of tea and bade them farewell with no 'charge' – in relation to either the hospitality or any offence. *Double Take* in turn gave way to *Bad Press* in 1986. Slowly, improvements were shown, for there was plenty of exciting sports news to report.

The new structures at Sketty Lane heralded a successful decade for sport. In 1980 the rugby club enjoyed an unbeaten tour of the Chicago, Milwaukee and Madison areas of the USA. The tourists had spent the previous year raising funds and one novel and activity that was reported in the *South Wales Evening Post* included a sponsored push of a wooden scrummage machine from Swansea to Twickenham with

The 1980s and 90s

the aim of arriving on the morning of an England v Wales international. Teams of pushers (including Ian Martineau, Rob Hopkins and Colin Jones) kept the weighty machine in a constant twenty-four hours a day motion along a route that avoided motorways. It was a rewarding if exhausting feat. In 1982 the 1st XV defeated other overseas opposition (at home) in the shape of the visiting Swedish national team and McGill University from Canada. There were also entertaining matches against first-class Welsh clubs and epic WRU Cup games against Tredegar and Newport.

During the latter part of the decade the rugby club found itself 'on the road to Twickers' again for the 1st XV reached three consecutive UAU finals, losing to their nemesis Loughborough on each occasion, no matter how spirited they performed under captains Lee Evans and Dinlle Francis. Each final was well supported by students, staff and alumni all enjoying a special day out. Amongst the latter was Haydn Tanner, doyen of UAU and Welsh rugby in the Thirties and honorary fellow of the University. The rugby club was blessed with 'strength in depth', for during the Eighties both the second and third XVs were crowned UAU champions. 1st XV captains included Steve Roberts, Mark Picton and Jon Gould. Much sage advice was forthcoming from the 'Trebanos Trio' – scrum half and captain Anthony Jones, forward Andrew 'Boris' Thomas and popular, non-playing mature student, father figure, counsellor and physio, the portly Clive Penhale.

A host of excellent players took part in University rugby and many earned places in representative teams such as the UAU and the newly-installed Wales Students and Wales Under 21 teams. Some reached the pinnacle by gaining international honours. "Thorburn makes Welsh XV" was a headline in *Double Take* in 1985. Paul Thorburn was a prolific scorer for the University 1st XV and Neath RFC. He went on to play for Wales thirty-seven times and was a committed and respected captain of his country. He remains a keen and helpful supporter of University sport. David Evans, David Bryant, Andy Moore and Mark Bennett also played for Wales. Bennett later became conditioning coach for the national team contributing to two Grand Slams in 2005 and 2008. He followed this with an appointment as head of sports science and medicine at the RFU. Andy Booth was selected for the Wales World Cup squad (1987) and both he and John Rowlands were chosen for the Wales B team. It was a particular pleasure for me to see four University alumni in the Wales squad during my time on the coaching staff of the national team during the late 1980s. Mark Schieffler (Canada) and Eduardo Macedo (Portugal) also represented their countries. Evans, Moore, Booth and Simon Bryant won blues at Oxbridge. In his post-University days, Matt Newman, after hanging up his rugby boots, joined David Evans on the staff at the SCW before moving on to become chief executive of Welsh Athletics. Evans later took up the post of international sports events manager for the Welsh Assembly Government (WAG).

The football club had mixed fortunes during the Eighties. Team successes were rare, but individuals shone through. In 1980-81 1st XI captain Robyn Jones was selected for the British Universities team and, in his post-University days, enjoyed a varied and successful career in coaching and academic life holding a professorship at Cardiff Metropolitan University. In 1982 the 2nd XI were victors in the UAU championship and in the following year all three teams won their UW competitions. However, in 1984-85 the club were demoted from the Welsh League where they had been playing since 1966-67. The decision was made due to administrative lapses on the part of the students. Despite an appeal and the commitment and efforts of secretary Mike Ede, protests were in vain. Ede expressed the view that: "... the University team was not popular with the League due to resentment against students, vacation problems and an application from Cardiff City reserves to fill any vacancy that should occur".

[4] Unfortunately the Welsh FA had its own opinion. While playing in the local Swansea league in 1988-89, Steve Norris, and Dean Herrity showed good enough form to be selected for the UAU, and 1st XI captain Phil Bowden represented the British Universities. The outstanding player of the decade was goalkeeper Mike Hooper who played for Bristol City and Wrexham before being signed by Liverpool manager Kenny Dalglish as an understudy for Bruce Grobbelaar. He was later transferred to Newcastle United for £550,000.

The hockey 1st XI topped the South Wales League Division One in 1981 and gained promotion to the Premier League. They were also UW champions on three occasions while the 2nd XI were successful in UW competition and reached a UAU final. Dave Baker (UAU), Ian McKenzie (Wales U21), Andy Palmer and Daniel Jones (Wales) were some of the outstanding players of the Eighties. Steve Rixon and Chris Rogers were hard-working captains while Kieron Dempsey, Graeme Bilsland and Guy Dale-Smith were amongst those who represented UW.

Rugby league grew in strength and the team reached the finals of the UCARLA and UAU competitions. They beat Oxford in a cup match at Central Park, Wigan, the heartland of the professional game in England. Special acclaim was reserved for Dr Phil Melling, a rugby league enthusiast on the staff of the American Studies department. He instilled much of his own passion, interest and enthusiasm in the players. Students who gained representative honours included Phil Waring, Stuart Madden, Lawrence Carr, Neil Cornforth and Graham Price.

There is plenty of evidence that women's sport was following the societal trends referred to earlier. During the first two years of the decade, women students entered five-a-side football teams into tournaments at Keele. However, it is thought that the first eleven-a-side team was not fielded until 1985-86 when Swansea played Cardiff. The Swansea girls won by 5-0 which included a "superb hat-trick from Cathy Weekes". It was claimed that the result "augurs well for the ladies game in Swansea". [5] In 1988-89 progress was confirmed when Swansea won UW and also beat Bristol by 5-0, which included another hat-trick from Alison Howes.

Women's rugby was developed in UK universities in the 1970s. Swansea's first competitive match was away against Aberystwyth in 1982-83 and resulted in a defeat by 8-0. [6] Swansea student Chris White refereed the game. Along with John Grice, he was also coach to the women's team. The result perhaps offers some early indication of White's impartiality for in his post-University days he became an outstanding referee under the Rugby Football Union (RFU). He officiated in more than fifty international matches including three World Cup tournaments.

In 1984-85 the women's team were finalists in a UAU competition at Keele. Cathy Murphy, Jane Talbot and Julia Owen were among the stalwarts of the time. 1987-88 was a significant year (referred to earlier) for Rhian Morgan, Gee Fen Paw, Sara Williams and Elaine Skiffington were all selected for the inaugural Wales women's team against England. Swansea student John Grice, himself a British Universities player, was the Welsh team's coach. The progress in women's rugby in Wales was becoming evident with a telling contribution from the University's players. The University's standing was further cemented when the Swansea women won the UAU tournament in 1988, a very creditable achievement considering the short existence of the club.

Women's basketball was founded in 1983 and by the end of the decade they were UW champions for the first time. In 1989-90 the volleyball club showed improvement when they reached the UAU finals at Birmingham and defeated Surrey, Warwick and Manchester. It was reported that: "the team created a general surprise especially amongst our competitors and UAU organisers".

The 1980s and 90s

Early in the decade the hockey club had some stand-out UAU players in Diane Spencer and Mandy Clifton while Debbie Robinson played for the British Universities. By the mid-Eighties Julie Wilson, Katharine Grant and Julie Dale were representing UW while Alison Watts and Joanne Ball earned selection for the British Universities team. Swansea were UW champions in 1988 under the captaincy of Ann Morris who was well supported by Debbie Jones, Ceri-Ann Painter and Maz Purcell, amongst others. However, the outstanding player of the decade was Emma James who became a Wales international and Commonwealth Games selection.

During the Eighties the lacrosse club, following a lapse of interest over a period of time, won the UW championship three times with Welsh international Rhian Morgan an inspiration and driving force.

BUSF player Susan Price, from Maesteg, served the netball club well in the early part of the decade. The club enjoyed tours to Jersey including one in 1984 when a report on the tourists claimed that: "Once more they have invaded Jersey, leaving it with only the sweet memories of their melodic singing and vivacious merry-making. Mad Jane played a prominent part in this year's little jaunt although her taste in sunglasses and drinks left much to be desired". [7] The following year memories of the light-hearted tour were partly fading when the reality of an over competitive home match against the Polytechnic of Wales brought controversy as: "... violent scenes led to the visitors' goal defence being sent from the game for unnecessary aggression". Who said that women are soft?

During the Eighties women excelled in racket sports. In the early years the tennis club carried off the UW championship three times and were UAU finalists in 1985-86. Alison Pardey and Graham Clark won the UAU mixed doubles tournament. Other outstanding players were Liz Charlton, Ann Underwood, Sarah Jane Hyde and Sue Mitchell who all represented the UAU. The latter went on to enjoy a successful career in education, becoming a headteacher at St John the Baptist Church in Wales High School in Aberdare. She was appointed MBE for services to her profession.

The badminton team were UW champions in 1982 and, towards the end of the decade, Jane Ashfold and Gee Fen Paw represented the UAU. In table tennis Lesley Tyler, Alison Jones and Alice Wall formed the team that won the UAU championship held at Durham. International Tyler was a stand-out player, becoming Welsh singles champion as well as winning UAU and BUSF titles.

Adopting changing attitudes nationwide, mixed gender teams were formed with selection earned on merit. In 1988-89 Val Hesketh became the first woman to represent the University in golf, joining the men in a fixture against Cardiff. In lifesaving Jackie Gill competed alongside four men in a tournament in Guernsey and helped the team win eight medals while in the same sport Jo Watt produced a 'stunning display of rope throwing' to help win another competition.

The women and men worked closely together in harriers and athletics events. Sarah Brownhill, Helen Collett, Louise Vaisey and Glenda Morris won the UW women's team race at Heath Park in Cardiff while the men competed in harriers' road relay charity events including a cross-country race in Germany. Colin Elvins and Glyn Thomas were keen competitors and the latter represented the UAU. Swansea dominated the UW athletics championships that were held successively at the Morfa Stadium and the Sketty Lane track in the early Eighties. Trinidadian Roger Monteil and Alison Preskey were inspirational captains and successful competitors. Preskey also won the BUSF heptathlon along with gold and silver medals at the UAU championships.

The outstanding athlete of the decade however was Neil Horsfield, a graceful runner in the 800m and 1500m events. He was European junior champion in 1985, became a Welsh record holder, and won the UK championship. Horsfield also represented GB in the World Student Games and Wales in two Commonwealth Games.

Another sport in which the women and men worked closely together was swimming. The Eighties proved a successful decade for the sport with Swansea eager to make a 'big splash' in national championships. Amongst the top performing women were Jackie Stanley, Alison Pryor, Wendy Evans, Liza Knott, Liz Coombs, Karen Smith, Liz Eggleton, Sam Walters and R Jackson, who were all UAU medallists. International swimmers included Sam Lewis (Wales), Stephanie Watson (Scotland) and Helen Walsh (England and GB). The latter became an 'All-American' scholar during her year abroad in the USA. The women's teams won UAU, BSSF and BUSF championships.

Amongst the men swimmers Tim Flintham was a hard-working captain and Tim Hayward a UAU medallist. By the mid Eighties Graeme Goudie, Andy Small, Andy Ambers, Sean Kinsey and Duncan Rolley were gold medallists at UAU and BUSF championships. Goudie (who also served a term as AU president) and Andy Rose swam for Scotland while Rolley represented England, GB and was a Commonwealth Games competitor. The men's team gained two runner-up places and two victories in UAU and BUSF championships.

Pool-based clubs often helped each other out in lifesaving, water polo and swimming competitions. In the early Eighties, the water polo club were UW champions three times with Tim Ford and Ian Barnes prominent. Wyn Bassett, Kevin Black and Adam Case represented UW. Early in the decade octopush was introduced as a new sport. It was a form of underwater hockey and involved snorkels, fins and a lead puck as equipment. By 1985-86 Joanne Talfound-Cooke had developed sufficiently to represent the UK.

At the sports hall, the basketball and volleyball clubs enjoyed their new facility. Basketball won two UW championships and volleyball made good progress. The latter won a home tournament against strong opposition from South Glamorgan Institute and Cardiff in 1981-2 and in the following year won the UW title for the first time, going on to reach the UAU finals.

In racket sports, the men could not match the team successes of the women in tennis but had an outstanding player in James Routledge who won the BUSF singles championship in 1988-89, the first player from a Welsh University to do so. He also represented GB in the World Student Games in Sheffield. Gavin Grant (badminton), Richard Parr and Chris Noakes (squash) were selected for the UAU. At the end of the decade, David Ayers, Simon Marten and Stuart Summers won a European squash tournament in Paris and this success was to be consolidated at the beginning of the next decade. Men's table tennis made an excellent start to the Eighties when Mark Pearson was captain. They went on to win UW on three occasions and reached the UAU semi-finals. The team went one better in 1984-5 under Tony Crook's leadership when they became UAU champions, beating Sheffield in the final. Both Crook and Jeremy Hobbs were also medallists in the UAU singles championships.

Amongst the smaller indoor clubs were fencing, archery, rifle and darts. Mustapha Baccouche represented the UAU in fencing and strove to maintain standards in the club. Alison Lewis won a UAU gold medal in archery. The rifle club had representation in the UW team and at the end of the decade Steve Conlon won a UW title. Women also played a part in the club with Gillian Curtis, Alison Bagley and Tracey Reader amongst the committed users of the shooting range at Fairwood, all endeavouring to improve standards in the precision sport.

Growing interest was shown in darts, another precision sport. In 1981 Iwan Rees was the University champion and the sport was being popularised by sponsorship from a beer company. The University team reached the final of the BUSA

The 1980s and 90s

darts championship in 1988-89, the venue being the Flying Whippet pub in Bristol. Swansea faced Loughborough, a University well-known for producing world record holders and Olympic medallists – though not in darts. With the incentive of generous supplies of beer as a prize, Swansea turned out winners, and as victory in any sport against such illustrious opponents was deserving of rejoicing: "... the jubilant team and supporters celebrated in style and spewed all the way home". [8]

Adopting a more serious approach, oceanography PhD student Steve Alexander made good use of the new weight training room. He formed a small training group at the Sports Centre consisting of himself, Steve Jones and Will Davies and specialised in powerlifting. Their training commitment led to a team victory in the BUSA powerlifting championships held at Strathclyde University in Scotland. Alexander was a dedicated competitor in the sport and entered British, European and World Championships. He won the gold medal in his category at the World Championships held in Calcutta in 1981 after two of his competitors were eliminated and banned for doping offences. Alexander's competitive and adventurous spirit stayed with him in his post-University days while living in America. He took up a research position at the Scripps Institute of Oceanography in San Diego and followed this with an around-the-world sailing challenge with his wife Jen, combining his passion for ocean travel, research and photography.

In the martial arts and combat sports, boxing 'took a dive' for little interest was shown in the activity during the decade. Karate became the 'trendy' martial art and attracted large numbers. Paul Davies captained the club and became its first black belt and Glen Hawkins represented Wales. They helped the club win the BSSF Championship. In 1984 the judo club, under the watchful eye of coach Terry Bennett won twenty-four from twenty-five bouts in the UW competition held at

Swansea. Sean York won gold and Andy Saywell bronze at the BUSF championship while Dawn Sherringham, Carol Jones, Helen Webb and Jane Van Dijk also won BUSF gold medals.

Aided by the new indoor nets at the Sports Centre, the cricket club built up a strong team spirit during winter practices. There was a group of excellent players who earned representative honours including Mike Cann (Glamorgan and Combined Universities), Julian Francis (UAU), Treharne Parker and Neil Pritchard (both Combined Universities). The two outstanding cricketers of the decade were Steve James and Adrian Dale. They provided the experience for a fine team effort in winning the UAU final against Durham in 1988. After defeating Manchester to reach the final for the first time, it was interesting to observe the proud and excited students beginning to celebrate with generous amounts of beer and the prospect of a late night at the hotel where they were staying before facing Durham the following day. However, both James and Dale set an example by consuming soft drinks and retiring to bed by 10pm in order to try and win the final the next day at the Derbyshire County Cricket ground. Thankfully, with a little prompting (and perhaps a touch of guilt), the rest of the team retired early too. Future England captain Nasser Hussein and Sussex county player Martin Speight were in the Durham side but could not prevent Dale scoring an unbeaten century and James hitting 86. John Williams contributed with 46 not out and this was enough (along with Dale's bowling figures of 4-64) to win Swansea the championship for the first time. The celebrations that had been delayed from the previous evening then began in earnest with the popping of champagne corks. James swopped Fairwood for Fenners after graduating and earned his blue at Cambridge. In his last innings as a student, he scored a century against New Zealand. He later played for England and with all-rounder Dale enjoyed a successful career in county cricket with Glamorgan. In 1993 the latter, while partnering West Indian star Viv Richards, put on a mammoth unbeaten stand of 425 between them against Middlesex at Sophia Gardens with the former student contributing 214. Dale now enjoys living and following a coaching career in New Zealand.

There was a growth of interest in outdoor activities, especially surfing, and Mike Schilling was chosen to represent Wales. PhD student Paul Russell was another outstanding surfer and won both the BUSF and European individual championships. He also inspired the surf club to win the BSSF competition. It was claimed that: "Paul is researching into wave-induced sediment transfer on high energy beaches; a topic which requires him to spend long hours monitoring waves on the beaches around Gower". [9] Perhaps a bit of a 'tongue-in-cheek' remark, but nevertheless, 'nice work if you can get it'.

The wind surfing, sailing, canoeing and sub-aqua clubs grew in numbers. Simon Brewer and Janet Best earned representative honours in sailing while the sub-aqua club flourished, aided by a new dedicated storage base and its own air compressor at the Sports Centre. The canoe club enjoyed visits to Llandysul, the Lake District and Scotland during which tours they experienced "copious amounts of beer and capsizes". In more serious mode Ian Howes (who served a term as AU president) and Angus Foley were selected for a BUSF kayak expedition to the river Zag in Turkey. The mountaineers made good use of the indoor climbing wall while the ski club organised annual trips to resorts in the French Alps.

The riding club won UW in 1984 when Sian Livesey gained first place and in 1988-89 Kim Belcher represented a British students' equestrian team at an event in the USA. Cycling was a newly-installed club with James Downton as one of its founders. In 1984-85 the clay pigeon shooting club participated in its first competitive fixture at Aberystwyth and used Fairwood as a home base. Lawrence Cogger, Pete Dickens and Stuart Connolly were early members and late in the decade James Stanton fulfilled sufficient promise to become a BUSF medallist.

Parachutists met at Fairwood Airport and towards the end of the Eighties students completed fourteen jumps in one day with debutantes Liz Vernon and Julie Edwards taking up the challenge. These two perhaps epitomised the more adventurous spirit of the decade amongst women, who were taking part in a broader range of activities. Such spirit went some way towards securing the UAU Winifred Clarke Trophy for the Swansea women for gaining most aggregate points in a range of UW and UAU competitions amongst small universities.

For the less adventurous, the new indoor facilities enabled a greater number and variety of voluntary instructional classes and by 1988-89 there was a choice of twenty-seven weekly activities. Amongst the more popular and colourful were the Monday and Thursday evening aerobics sessions taught by Gwyneth that attracted up to eighty to ninety students and staff to the sports hall floor with almost as many watching from the balcony. Each warm-up session started with Dire Strait's catchy 'Let's Dance' – a tune that still resonates with me (and I am sure many others) as a regular musical feature of student activity during those evenings.

In 1985-86 a Health and Fitness Unit was established for exercise assessment and prescription and it was well patronised by students and staff.

Numbers taking part in intramural sport also grew with ten sports offered each year on a league or tournament basis. The indoor five-a-side football league grew from forty-four teams to eighty. Irish Ghosts were victors in an early final that revealed a: "mixture of skill, maturity, thuggery and persistence". [10] Initially a series of mishaps occurred (including broken legs) in fiery competition and over-zealousness. This was eventually tempered and the tournament remained an annual favourite.

Eleven-a-side football, rugby sevens, basketball and

The 1980s and 90s

volleyball were well supported. The Biology Society, the National Union of Iraqi Students (NUIS) and the Greek Society were amongst the winners. There were forty-eight entries for a mixed-doubles tennis tournament in 1982-83 and forty-two entered the inter-hall table tennis event. Squash tournaments saw many staff-student battles and amongst the latter, Chris Noakes and Richard Parr were worthy winners in successive years. In 1985-86 the squash 'plate' competition was won by: "... the oldest entrant, wily lecturer Dr John Watson, of the electrical engineering department". In 1980-81 an annual lunchtime Turkey Trot Fun Run was founded for team and individual races. It took place over a three-and-a-half mile course at Sketty Lane attracting up to seventy runners. Individual winners included Paul Timblick and Sarah Brownhill.

Every summer after examinations, an annual sports week was held. It often involved charity fundraising and fancy dress events. Guests and local sports celebrities also took part. A sum of £1,100 was collected for Sports Aid during one such week. In 1986 Lord Callaghan, the University president and the only 20th century politician to hold the "four great offices of state", presented the prizes. During a tour of the facilities, he related to me an interesting tale linking sport and politics emanating from dealings he had with the Ugandan president and dictator Idi Amin in the 1970s. On his tour of the Sports Centre, I led him to the swimming pool and he remarked: "Ah, this pool reminds me of a story linking sport and politics". He then went on to say that when he was Foreign Secretary in Harold Wilson's government in 1975, Idi Amin, the Ugandan dictator, had arrested a British subject Denis Wills, a college lecturer in Kampala. Wills was a fiercely outspoken critic of Amin's rule and was charged, imprisoned and sentenced to death by firing squad. The issue received widespread international publicity and Lord Callaghan explained that he was dispatched to Kampala by Harold Wilson to meet Amin and resolve the situation in order to prevent more serious diplomatic tension. On arriving in Kampala with some apprehension about how he would be received by the unstable dictator, he was reasonably surprised. Lord Callaghan went on to describe how when he stepped from the plane Amin was there to greet him and his first words were: "James Callaghan, MP for Cardiff, I have been there and swam in the Empire Pool ... don't worry about Mr Wills, I won't execute him". It transpired that Amin, while living in London some time previously, was a serious swimmer hoping to be selected for the Ugandan national team. He had visited Cardiff to train in the Olympic-sized pool. Lord Callaghan said that he was completely taken aback but it was all to his relief and from then on, he always associated swimming pools with the unpredictable General Amin and that diplomatic affair.

As might be imagined there were many requests from community groups and organisations for use of the facilities. One in particular came from the Australian cricket team whose match against Glamorgan at St Helen's was interrupted by rain for a full day. The team was granted use of the indoor cricket nets and other facilities. "Aussie sports stars at the Sports Centre" was a headline in *Double Take*. Trevor Chappel demonstrated his all-round skills in badminton, squash and volleyball competitions by performing well in each activity while tour captain Kim Hughes and wicket keeper legend Rodney Marsh also enjoyed the action. The Australian team manager Fred Bennett showed his appreciation when he stated that: "There's nothing to match these facilities 'Down Under' ... and I've seen nothing as good in the UK either ... the whole team is grateful for the cooperation given us by the staff here at the Sports Centre". [11] A little overblown in praise perhaps, but nevertheless a generous compliment and perceivably an appropriate comment on which to close the Eighties. The 'leap forward' consolidated sport and led to partnerships and further progress in the following decade.

The 1990s

THE NINETIES saw Margaret Thatcher replaced by John Major as prime minister. Tony Blair succeeded Major as the country's leader in 1997 with his New Labour mantra and remained in office until 2007. During his time in power, devolution government was granted to Wales and Scotland and progress made on the Northern Ireland peace process. Both Major and Blair introduced policies that changed education, thus affecting universities and in turn University sport.

Education reforms included the target setting of thirty per cent of school leavers encouraged to enter higher education, indicating a move from an elite to a mass arrangement. In 1992 the binary system was abolished allowing polytechnics to be transformed into universities. Following on from the previous decade there were more challenges like further overseas recruitment, crowded facilities, semesterisation, modular degree schemes, new courses and funding issues. The introduction of the Quality Assessment Agency (QAA) and student loans were other changes. At Swansea, new courses in nursing, law and sports science were introduced, more of which later.

Universities saw the rise of the worldwide web, email and faxes. It was also an age of public relations and 'management speak' while fashion amongst students included the wearing of bandanas, back-to-front baseball caps, tattoos and body piercing. Celebrity culture embraced the music of bands like Oasis and the University's own Manic Street Preachers. Popular TV sitcoms included 'Father Ted' and 'The Royle Family' while films such as 'Jurassic Park' and 'The Full Monty' attracted cinemagoers.

An important factor impacting on sport nationally (that eventually benefited Swansea) was the founding of the National Lottery in 1994. It brought funding for the development of new and the upgrading of older facilities. In 1996 it was also decided to fund elite athletes and establish a British Academy for Sport along the lines of the successful Australian Institute of Sport (AIS). It eventually arrived in the form of the United Kingdom Institute of Sport (UKIS) based at Sheffield. Prime minister John Major, himself an ardent sports follower, stated that: "I knew there was no chance of funding the long-term development of sport and the arts from general government revenue. A lottery could do just that".

In 1995 the government's vision for sport was published in a document titled: 'Sport: Raising the Game'. In it, John Major claimed that: "Sport is a central part of Britain's heritage ... we should cherish it". With special reference to universities he went on to say that: "Students should continue to have opportunity to develop a lifelong interest in recreational or competitive sport". He welcomed the growing interest in sports studies courses and a wider spread of best practice in sports scholarships. [1] The issue of combining academic and sporting excellence was discussed and debated in the national press and sports magazines.

Scott Moffatt, the University 1st XI cricket captain, joined the debate and aired his views on Oxbridge cricket and the pecking order for university teams. He placed Swansea in third place behind Oxford and Durham. It was claimed by others that good cricketers were attracted to Swansea as they knew the University took its sport seriously and had the added incentive of sports scholarships. [2]

The whole question was taken up at government level and Sports Minister Ian Sproat declared that: "I want to see more scholarships to help our top athletes ... and ways of recognising and celebrating their sporting achievements". In 1995 esteemed former athlete and distinguished neurosurgeon Sir Roger Bannister was appointed to chair a working group on the subject. [3] I was invited to join the group, along with a small selection of other university directors of sport, academics and personnel with international sporting experience. Bannister stated that: "Our working group tackles

Official opening of the new Sports Centre 1981. Lord Hunt and Principal Steel

Archdeacon H. Williams, Principal Steel, Lord Hunt, Judge Rowe Harding, Professor Ieuan Williams

John Palmer, Principal Steel, Lord Hunt, Stan Addicott, Gwyneth John (later Diment)

New Sports Hall

Steve Alexander training in the Weights Room 1980s

Climbing wall

Women's hockey mid 1980s (Julie Wilson capt)

Women's rugby UAU Champions 1985-86

1st XI football early 1980s (Declan Jordan capt)

1st XV UAU Rugby Union Final at Twickenham late 1980s

Staff support at Twickenham 1980s

Rugby 3rd XV UAU Champions 1989-90

UAU 1st XI cricket champions 1988. (Adrian Dale and Steve James padded up)

BUSA 1st XI cricket champions 1993-94 (Scott Moffatt, capt)

UAU Squash champions 1992-93

Paul Thorburn and boots worn for the 'kick of the age' against Scotland 1986

Swansea captain receiving the BUSA cup from Princess Anne

BUSA 1st XV rugby champions 1998-99 (Ben Martin capt)

BUSA 1st XV rugby champions 1997-98 (Ben Williams capt)

Victory celebrations at Twickenham 1997-98

Rugby club lunch. Staff members and 8 alumni internationals. Late 1990s

'Sweaty sports are just not feminine'

Singing, swearing, drinking and more than a match for the rugby men

THE bar-room talk in Llanharan was of how Hughie Price lost his trousers.

The Welsh village may be used to the rowdy pranks of rugby players, but this time it was different.

"It was the best night he's ever had," said barmaid Sue Welsh. "We are used to the men going crazy after matches, but the women really got stuck in as well. It was a great atmosphere.

"They were knocking back the pints after Monday's match. Some of them had 10.

"And you should have heard the language — swearing like troopers."

Whatever the comparisons between men's and women's rugby, the after-match rituals appear to answer insignificant details like gender.

The first ever Women's Rugby World Cup, hosted by Wales, has proved to be a roaring, staggering success off the pitch as well as on it.

Rugby clubs at all the tournament venues have had to admit that when it comes to the game's noisy traditions the women are more than a match for the men.

World Tournament spokeswoman Alice Cooper said men did not have the sole rights to post match enjoyment.

"All the 12 teams, she said, from countries as far as Japan and Russia, were enjoying

Glamorgan on Wednesday, local rugby club chairman Malcolm Hall, 41, said: he would welcome the women back any time.

they are women. They haven't got the strength and stamina but they have got all the right ideas," he said.

But despite their disappointing defeat, they slipped in a couple of pints and managed a few bars of Welsh song.

In response, the All Blacks produced a guitar and had a group singalong which swept ideas about what happens after a game.

Canadian captain Ruth Hellerud-Brown, 3, and vice-captain Stephanie White, 29, said they tried to avoid the more extreme modes of expression.

"But that doesn't mean we regarded as a man's game," said Stephanie.

"And we don't get rugby groupies following us around, damn it! Men are more likely to come up to us after a game to tell us what we'd done wrong."

PLUCKY: Victorious Kiwis find cause for celebration in the bar at Llanharan clubhouse

Words: Helen Weathers Pictures: Lynne McEwan

FULL FLIGHT: Kiwi prop Ericka Rere in action

Cynical headlines regarding women's sport 1991

Michelle Owen, Sky Sports football presenter late 2010

Tanni Grey-Thomson awarded an Honorary Fellowship

Liz Johnson awarded an Honorary Fellowship

arah Powell awarded an
lonorary Doctorate

SCHOLARSHIPS

TALENTED ATHLETE SCHOLARSHIP SCHEME

TASS logo

Gareth Lewis

Tim Dykes

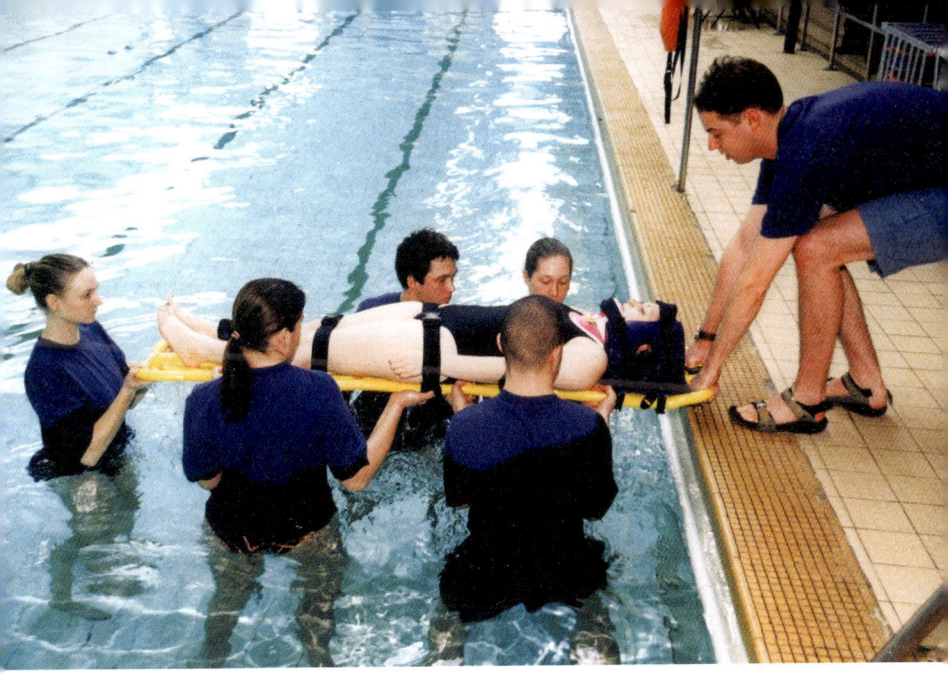

Life saving training at the old pool 2003

Presentation to the Sports Centre staff by the STA 2003

Presentation by Gwyneth at Sport Swansea Awards dinner

Renee Godfrey, Wa and BUCS surfing champion (c2000)

Rowing club pose for charity calendar 2010

Canoe club in Swansea Bay

Welsh Varsity logo

Men's hockey (Shield match)

Men's teams line up at the
Millennium Stadium (Varsity Cup)

Women's netball (Shield match)

Women's rugby (Shield match)

Swansea Sirens

INTRA-MURAL SPORT 1980-90s

Fancy dress Fun Run

Fun Run start

Staff Fun Run winners

Rugby Sevens winners

PGCE PHYSICAL EDUCATION

FAW Award course 1990

Derek Peaple (Olympic Legacy Award 2012)

'Spreading the gospel'

Rock climbing at Dolygae

Modest East End maths teacher and Essex schoolboys cricket coach

Haydn Davies, 84

The Essex cricket coach and east London maths teacher Haydn Davies was not one to relish the limelight or celebrate his achievements. The long-service glass plaque from the English Schools Cricket Association that was presented to him in 2014 by two former Essex schoolboys, Stephen Peters and Nasser Hussain, was promptly dropped in the car park that evening and smashed. He was not unduly concerned. Invited to receive an award at Lord's for what he assumed would be a small affair, he was surprised to find a marquee of 250 people in black tie, and the speakers were Brian Johnston, Denis Compton and Leslie Crowther. The winners included the England skippers Alec Stewart and Rachael Heyhoe Flint — and Haydn.

As a committee member of the Essex County Schools Cricket Association for more than 50 years, Haydn Davies devoted his time to helping others to succeed in the game. He rarely took a day off, even in the summer holidays, and at the height of his energy in the 1980s was organising 100 matches a year for Essex schoolboys. His commitment to the county paid dividends. Several top players emerged through the Essex schools association, including the future England captains Alastair Cook and Nasser Hussain, as well as Ravi Bopara, Neil Foster, James Foster and Paul Prichard.

Twinning his love of cricket with maths teaching, Haydn spent his entire career in Newham, east London. He started out at the Thomas Lethaby secondary modern in East Ham before moving in 1959 to the East Ham Grammar School for Boys. In his first year he was proud to have taught Ronnie Boyce, who scored the winning goal for West Ham United in the 1964 FA Cup final.

In 1972 the schools amalgamated to form the 2,000-strong Langdon Comprehensive, where Haydn stayed until 1993. He had dedicated his life to teaching in an era when he could flourish without having to follow onerous health and safety regulations and harsh accountability regimes. The writing was probably on the wall for him the first time his school was inspected. He was asked how he communicated with his department. "It's simple," he said. "I go and talk to them." He retired shortly after, preferring to concentrate his efforts

Haydn Davies with the former England captain Nasser Hussain, left, in 2014

Bishopston Centre manager Emma Evans joined by Freedom Leisure managing director Ivan Horsfall-Turner (right) and head of Bishopston Comprehensive School Jeff Bird (left).

Leisure centres' facilities given an upgrade

given his first teaching position. Popular with his pupils, he kitted out his large maths store room with a Prince's rugby team and, as their fortunes fluctuated, liked to employ a favourite phrase: "Nil desperandum (Never despair)."

an important sector of 1.5 million university students at the age crucial for developing sporting talent. By the year 2000 approximately half of the British Olympic team is expected to be or have been in higher education, so we should plan now". He also argued that there should be no conflict between academic work and sport for with careful planning success could be achieved in both. [4]

By this time Swansea (along with a number of other universities such as Bath and Stirling) had been operating a scholarship programme for ten years and enjoyed partnerships with the Royal and Ancient Golf Club (R&A) and the Swansea Rugby Foundation who provided scholarships in addition to those of the University. Meanwhile in Wales, government funding for elite athletes gained via the Lottery was channeled through the newly-created UK Sports Council (1994) to the SCW. The latter decided to fund individuals through the Athlete Career Education (ACE) and Elite Cymru Sportlot Award schemes rather than support institutions directly. [5] The efforts of the Bannister Working Group bore fruit in 2002 when the Talented Athlete Scholarship Scheme (TASS) was announced, and this will be explained in due course.

Nationally there was a culture of commercialism, sponsorship, Sky TV, media profile and celebrity status pervading sport. Universities were obliged to adjust, change and innovate. In 1993, due to the ending of the binary system referred to earlier, professional sports staff in universities and polytechnics formed the British Universities and Colleges Physical Education Association (BUCPEA). The following year saw the British Universities Sports Association (BUSA) replace the UAU and BUSF to organise student sport. This saw the demise of the UW championships (that had been in existence since the 1920s) for, going forward, competition was to be structured across the country in the form of premier leagues and conferences. Successive AU presidents at Swansea worked hard to keep pace with progress. A senior staff change at the Sports Centre saw Kevin Harrison replace Paul Hickson as assistant director.

As well as keeping up with change, the AU was prepared to innovate. In 1993-94 president Gethin Jenkins organised a first-ever weekend ferry trip to Cork University for 200 sports people. According to reports it was a success on and off the fields of play despite the fact that: "... many teams staggered straight from the very rough (and drunken) ferry journey onto court". There were seven wins, five draws and three losses recorded by the fifteen travelling teams. Jenkins's organisational skills stood him in good stead in his future career in sports administration when he took up a position with the IRB followed by roles of chief executive at Newport Gwent Dragons Rugby, Cardiff City FC and England Boxing.

Meanwhile, there were other developments that had implications for student sport and alumni. The game of rugby union turned professional in 1995. Four outstanding Swansea University players Andrew Lewis, Dafydd James, Dwayne Peel and Stephen Jones (who was to play over 100 times for his country) were lured away from their University courses by the monetary and other attractions of the new professional game. All became Welsh international players and the latter three represented the British and Irish Lions. On retirement from playing, some enjoyed successful chosen careers, but Dafydd later publicly expressed regret at not being able to adapt properly to mainstream life following his stellar rugby career. He intimated that he could have planned better for his life after rugby. However, at that time in the newly-professionalised sport, there was little guidance, advice or support available from the governing body for young players' futures after their playing days were over. Other less talented University players were able to play semi-professional rugby for clubs and turn out for University teams. Wales hosted the 1999 Rugby World Cup and alumnus Paul Thorburn was the successful tournament director.

The 1980s and 90s

For the University rugby club 'the road to Twickenham' opened up again. During the Nineties the University 1st XV reached four UAU/BUSA finals, being victorious on two occasions. Early in the decade, narrow defeats were suffered against Cardiff (despite the promptings of skipper Richard Mynott) and West London Institute (now Brunel University). Regarding the latter match, rugby journalist Stephen Jones writing in *The Sunday Times* mentioned that: "I did see one outstanding performance by a Welsh team last week, in the British Universities final at Twickenham ... where in injury time Swansea were unfathomably penalised and West London won with the last kick of the match. Swansea players fell to the ground as if poleaxed ... the team had been mugged". Rhodri Griffiths's team scored four tries to one and "two seemingly legitimate scores were disallowed". [6] Later in the decade the defeats were avenged against Northumbria University and St Mary's University College under successive captains, Ben Williams and Ben Martin. Williams's team's win earned the headline: "Swansea success ends that final jinx at last" – a reference to the fact that the University had played in seven losing Twickenham finals before that day. After the victory over St Mary's, BUSA patron Princess Anne was in attendance to present the trophy to the winning Swansea captain. Of Martin's triumph the *Western Mail* reported that: "There have not been many victories for Welsh teams at Twickenham in recent years so the efforts of Swansea University should be applauded and acknowledged by the nation they represented with such style". [7] During a special day for many in London, the 2nd XV also won their final against Nottingham when Pete Mannion led the team.

A new addition to the rugby playing programme, in which Swansea performed creditably, was the launch of a Student European Rugby Cup competition (SERC) sponsored by *The Times* newspaper. Also, in 1997 the first annual Welsh Varsity match was played against Cardiff with the aim of raising funds for Oxfam. During a subsequent season, the Varsity match was played at St Helen's and the AU president upped the crowd atmosphere with accompanying music, fireworks and half-time entertainment. The latter included two male 'streakers' painted in the livery of their team and as they boldly hastened across the field the announcer on the public address system was heard to comment: "That's the worst tackle I've seen all night!"

Adopting a more serious approach to the game, Richard Smith, Ian Buckett, Rob Howley (future Wales captain, British Lion, international coach and honorary fellow of the University) and David Weatherley all went on to play for Wales. Former Kelly College pupil and Nigeria-born Adedayo Adebayo represented England and Chris Clark, England B. Prop forward Clark, who had captained the University 1st XV appeared for the All Whites in his final year and played in a momentous victory over world champions Australia at St Helen's in 1992. Despite his lack of experience at that level it was reported that: "... the young Clark performed as if he were a seasoned international".

A unique contribution to the rugby club during this era came from the three Langley brothers of St Cyres School, Penarth. Mark, Colin and Paul all packed down in the scrum at different times in the course of the decade, provided stalwart service and earned representative honours. Eleven students moved to Oxbridge during the Nineties to win blues. Buckett, Clark, Gareth Baber, Richard Jones and Andy Collins represented the 'dark blues' while Simon Bryant, Paul Flood, Richard Dix, Neil Hennessey, Andrew Grabham and James Meredith donned the 'light blue' shirt. During his Swansea days, prop forward Meredith – known to his team-mates as 'gas-man', probably due to his speed around the pitch – was 1st XV captain. He gained a first-class honours degree before progressing to Cambridge, thus helping to dispel the myth that those who played in the dark, mysterious confines of the

The 1980s and 90s

front row of the scrum must be lacking in grey matter. Baber, during his later coaching career, travelled further afield when he took charge of the Fiji Rugby Sevens team in preparation for the Tokyo Olympics in 2020. His hard work, coupled with the magic skills of the Fijian players helped secure the gold medal for the Pacific islanders.

Nationally, football was revitalised in 1992-93 with the formation of the FA Premier League aided by the riches of Sky TV. With less heralding, the National League of Wales was also formed and offered a route to European football for successful teams. The riches of the sport did not shower down upon the students but amongst the University players Steve Norris, Paul Cronin, Cameron Toshack and Richard Pratley were prominent early in the decade. Andrew Varley, Paul Underwood, David Birch and Andy Pitman were strong players and loyal clubmen. In later years Toshack (son of the revered John) moved into football management and played a key role in developing talent for Swansea City FC. Pratley enjoyed a career in the RAF reaching the rank of Air Commodore in the Ministry of Defence. Towards the end of the decade a suspect attitude in the student club was revealed when a team official was asked to sum up his club in one sentence during a *Waterfront* interview. He said: "No one likes us and we don't care". However, elected captain Martyn Williams, who gained a 'first' as one of the initial cohort of students undertaking the new Sports Science degree, worked hard to change the culture of the football club. Consequently, a better spirit was revealed before the end of the Nineties.

In cricket, Glamorgan won the county championship in1997. Alumnus Steve James was the country's leading run-maker, scoring 1,775 runs and his former University team-mate, all-rounder Adrian Dale, also played a big part in the county's triumph. The University had an eventful and successful decade reaching semi-finals and finals in six- and eleven-a-side competitions. The outstanding performance was in 1993 when the 1st XI beat Durham in the BUSA final. History students Grant Humphreys and Duncan Verrey both scored half centuries while bowlers Nick Davies and Scott Moffatt helped skittle out the Durham batsmen. Amongst those who stood out during the Nineties was prolific scorer Gul Khan who afterwards undertook a post-graduate course at Oxford and won his blue. He ended his Oxford season with an average of over fifty runs and later played county cricket for Derbyshire. James Langworth represented Wales Minor Counties twenty-seven times and Dan Cherry had a brief career for Glamorgan, scoring three centuries and a career best of 226 against Middlesex. He now serves on the county staff as operations manager at the SWALEC stadium. Others who gave loyal service to the University club during the period include Dave Bowen, Mike Williamson, Andy Law, Carl Lawrence, Kafeel Jahangir, Maleth Madurasinghe, Ian Gompertz, Richard Howitt, David Barr and Stuart Morris.

Across the country, track and field athletics increased its profile and popularity. The sport was transformed by exposure to television, trust funds, appearance money and sponsorship. Colin Jackson, Jamie Baulch, Iwan Thomas and Tanni Grey-Thompson flew the flag for Wales. The University had its own star in law student Daniel Caines who became a world 400m indoor record holder, Commonwealth Games 400m relay gold medallist and double Olympian at Sydney (2000) and Athens (2004). On his selection for the Sydney Olympics, which came only weeks after his final examinations, his lecturer Richard Townshend-Smith commented that: "This is an impressive achievement for any young man but to be able to combine studying for a degree with athletic success at this level is truly admirable". [8] Louise Whitehead was another successful athlete. She was Welsh champion over a three-year period in the 200m, 400m, and 400m hurdles. Whitehead also represented GB in the World Student Games and was a BUSA silver medallist. The University harriers team was also well served by sisters Jane and Alison Finney. The club won the West Glamorgan League and was voted AU Club of the Year in 1997.

During the Nineties golf received much public attention in Wales, sparked by the form of Ian Woosnam who won the US Masters, held twenty-nine European titles and was first in the world rankings. Wales had seven golfers in the PGA European 100 list and many new golf courses were opened during the decade. Interest was reflected in the universities and generous sponsorship in the form of the Royal & Ancient (R&A) Foundation Bursary Scheme came to Swansea. Early in the decade the golf team won UW on two occasions and reached the UAU semi-finals. Neil Allen and Julie Wilson (a BUSA medallist), Aaron Wilde, Nick Collier and David Janskewski stood out while Dr Simon Jenkins (Director of Sports Science from 1997-2000) nurtured interest. Team captain Gareth Lewis forged a promising career in the golf world, holding positions as a coach educator for the Professional Golf Association (PGA), golf manager at the Belfry GC and head professional and manager at Royal Harlech GC.

Women's sport continued to grow and hockey in Wales was exceptionally well served by local figure Anne Ellis from Gowerton who played 136 times for Wales, captained her country and GB. She became a future chair of the Wales National Pool (WNP) and an honorary fellow of the University. The Nineties were a successful time for University hockey in UW and UAU competitions. Some outstanding players came through the ranks of the University women's club including Nicola Donald who represented Wales and GB in the World Student Games in Sheffield. Describing her time at the games, she stated: "It was a fantastic experience to represent my country ... Walking into the stadium with 25,000 screaming fans all chanting 'Great Britain, Great Britain'... was probably the crowning moment". [9]

Sarah Powell was another stand-out player. She won over

seventy caps for Wales, captained and coached her country, and took part in the Commonwealth Games in Kuala Lumpur in 1998. Her professional career led to her becoming the first female chief executive officer (CEO) for Sport Wales. She was presented with an honorary doctorate by the University and on receiving her award claimed that: "To be back in Swansea, where I have so many great memories of both studying and playing sport, makes the day and the recognition even more special". [10]

Women's rugby and football were fast-growing sports and gaining public attention although they were more participative than a magnet for spectators. In 1991 Wales hosted the inaugural Women's Rugby World Cup with twelve countries participating. The University women's team found it difficult to hold onto the success of the Eighties but in 1992-93 the first UW representative side was fielded against the Midlands Universities with five from Swansea in the team including captain Karen Williams. The Swansea women were impressed that the match was played at Loughborough on the men's 1st XV pitch and hinted that a similar experience for the Swansea team at Sketty Lane would be appreciated. However, five years later, a report from 1998-99 by Maria Gough indicated that there was a good victory at Sketty Lane by the women's team against Glamorgan and that it was the first time that the women had played there. Was there some unconscious bias against the women that deprived them of the best University rugby facility for so long? This writer feels some guilt. [11]

Women's football was gaining more profile too in Wales. In 1993 the game was 'officially' founded and the first international match was arranged – although women had played for many years before this time. Barry Ladies FC were promoted to the FA Women's Premier League, competing against the likes of Arsenal and Everton. Moving into the following decade there were approximately fifty senior teams in the country and twelve active referees. [12] In 1992-93 publicity for the

The 1980s and 90s

University's women's club centered around a sponsored head-shave in the Mandela bar to raise funds for the Swansea Aids Charity. Nikki and Julia were the 'stooges' but there was no evidence to show that their speed improved on the playing field (if that was to be a wish) as was the case for swimmers in the pool who shed their body hair. Rachel Willock was a prolific scorer for the women's team with two hat-tricks in successive matches.

Some cynicism and prejudice surrounded women's participation in the above sports and media reports were not always kind. "Sweaty sports are not feminine" was one newspaper column headline and: "Singing, swearing, drinking and more than a match for the rugby men" another. The Sports Council for Wales fought back with an article headed: "Women's sport needs serious treatment" in an attempt to prevent girls from dropping out of physical activities. [13] The progress of women's sport will be further discussed later.

At the University, amongst women, there was more success for individuals than teams. Karen Phillips and Jo Morton excelled at squash. Alex Bennett (cricket), Debbie Howarth (trampoline), Tracey Murray (archery), Liz Wildin (netball), Jane Duggan (netball) and Helen Barry (basketball) all gained representative honours or won medals. New sports undertaken included biathlon (running and swimming) in which the women gained second place behind Loughborough in the BUSA championships. Kylie Mansfield, Sue Hanscombe, Justine Williamson and international exchange student Maria-Theresa Zouzonki (referred to as 'Greece Lightning') formed the team. Women's lacrosse encouraged a mixed team and from this the men formed their own club.

High standards were set at the swimming pool where men and women students trained closely together. Swansea won the UAU President's Cup with Viv Clement (who served a term as AU president), Angela Knowles, Emma Knott, Ben Winter, Glen Hall and Brendan Bush forming the team. Ex-

Olchfa School pupil Victoria Hale, and Martyn Davies (son of alumnus Howard Davies, Olympian of the Sixties) swam for Wales in the Commonwealth Games in Kuala Lumpur. Davies also topped off his University days with a first-class degree in economics. Other Welsh internationals included Gary Morgan, Scott Reasons, Steve Evans, Mirelle Evans and siblings Mark and Sue Hanscombe. Simon Davies and Al Duke were BUSA medallists. Due to its success, the swimming club was voted AU Club of the Year in 1997-98.

The lifesaving club always made its presence felt in and out of the water, combining serious competition with fun challenges. Following a competition in Southampton they won beer-drinking 'boat and funnel' races with "consummate ease". A new beach lifesaving club sought to attract members by issuing a recruitment statement declaring that: "We are the only club where mouth-to-mouth technique has to be worked on regularly". However, the humanitarian nature of the sport was never neglected and students annually earned National Aquatic Rescue Standard (NARS) gold awards following training at the pool. Indeed, recognition of the work undertaken by the pool staff (Kevin Harrison, Brian Williamson and Roger Harvey) as well as that of students was shown when the Swimming Teachers Association (STA) presented an award to the University for the high standard of its work.

Outside the pool, men's hockey had a varied programme. Early in the decade they won an indoor UW tournament and proceeded to the UAU semi-final. Ed Haulk, James Edington, Richard Alban and Andy Edwards helped to provide the spine of a competitive club. Edwards moved on to Oxford to win his blue and afterwards forsook the hockey pitch for a challenging expedition to the Himalayas. The 1st XI won the South Wales League shield with Bastian Van Drempt scoring the winning goal, and under captain Matt Heslop they were also finalists in the Welsh cup at Sophia Gardens, Cardiff in 1998-99. Reward for their competitiveness came with a place in a European

The 1980s and 90s

Cup Winners competition in Vienna.

Early in the Nineties, the basketball club won UW and reached the South Wales League plate final when Mansel Rees and Steve Minney took up the positions of coach and captain. James Stevenson and Christos Oustaglou were prominent club members, but the team had to wait until the end of the decade for their best season when they reached the BUSA finals before losing to Oxford.

The 1992-93 season saw the outstanding racket sport success of the decade when the men's squash team won the UAU championship, beating Loughborough in the final at Bath University. Stuart Summers, Jason Martin, Dave Ayerst, Paul Barrell and Matthew Rudd formed the team. Team captain Martin stated in Bad Press that: "... our thanks go to Sports Centre staff Gwyneth, Stan and Geoff (of the electrical engineering department) who turned up to watch, for it has taken four years of their unprecedented support and encouragement to achieve this success". Team-mates later became antagonists when Rudd defeated Barrell in the UW singles championship final, but friendship was soon restored.

Of the martial arts, taekwondo was a newly-formed club and for the first time a team was entered into a UK open competition. Judo players competed regularly in national competitions with black belt Chris Langley always an inspiration while Helen Kelly, Becky Bushrod and Tregaron's Myfanwy Williams set standards for the ladies. The latter suffered a serious knee injury while competing during her year abroad in France but on her return was gratifyingly consoled after gaining a first-class honours degree in languages. Karate exponents Louise Brown, Tanya Morris, Lloyd Strawbridge and Steve Treavett achieved success in tournaments as did Thomas Stalze, Anthony Startup and Delphine Thullez in jiu jitsu.

In the 'adventurous' outdoor sports some activities declined while others grew. There was a lack of interest in clay pigeon shooting and despite enthusiast Chris Hudson's efforts in orienteering that sport flagged too. Indoor competitions in 'bouldering' – a branch of mountaineering that concentrated on: "strenuous and fiendishly tricky climbs leading to some fantastic falls onto the crash mats" – became popular. The 'free-falling' did not deter adherents such as Ellie Milledge, Steve Hodges, Dave Lucas, Neil Mullinger, Tom Silsbury and Donna Carless, who were among those who enjoyed the sport. A proliferation of dry ski slopes nationwide saw the introduction of leagues and competitions for students and annual snow trips were well subscribed by student club members. The rowing club enjoyed visits to York, Monmouth and Cardiff for regattas and co-operation was sought with Mumbles Rowing Club to promote the activity. In 1995-96 the men celebrated a victory over Cardiff at Monmouth in the 'coxed four'. Mark Proctor, Owain Evans, Mark Earnshaw and captain Andy John provided the muscle while Jenny Hobbs acted as cox. During his time as AU president, John did much to promote, raise standards and develop the sport.

Early in the decade the sailing club won the UW championship with David Boffey and Hannah Stancliffe prominent. During the following years a group of top-class sailors formed the competitive base of the club. Ian Clingan was selected for the UK in the Laser World Championships in New Zealand. In his post-University days, he went on to enjoy a successful sailing career and acted as one of the GB coaches at the Beijing Olympics. Daniel Newman won a BUSA gold medal. Towards the end of the decade, successive club captains, Duncan Truswell, Ian Fox and Danny Sanders, along with Ben Rhodes, David Smith and Welsh international Siân Reynolds, were competitive club stalwarts. Such was the standard of the club team that they were chosen en bloc to compete for the Welsh universities in the Student Yachting World Challenge Cup held in France.

Surfing maintained its popularity and two Irish champions

Andrew Hill and Zoe Lally represented their country in world championships in Puerto Rico and Japan respectively. Zoe also won first place in the BSSF women's championships. The surf club held annual events at Nolton Haven in Pembrokeshire, and at the end of the Nineties the men's and women's teams won the BUSA championships at Newquay, Cornwall against an entry of 300 competitors. Windsurfers Tom Williams, Simon Pearce and Tristan Boxford held national rankings and Duncan Mosley was a BUSA medallist. The canoe club was famed for eventful away trips to slalom and white water competitions, enjoying both the challenges of the rivers and the social atmosphere. In 1998-99 the club were active locally when they took advantage of heavy rain and storms to paddle around the flooded fairways of the Mond Valley Golf Club, Clydach, when the River Tawe broke its banks during the torrential rainfall – not an everyday route for the paddlers. Canoe polo, korfball, street and roller hockey were other new sports undertaken by the students.

In addition to club sports intramural competitions, recreational classes and coaching award courses were again well subscribed. Hendrefoilan Village students organised a five-a-side football competition at the newly-installed multi-purpose games area and the final of the MWL football was played at the Morfa Stadium to increase its profile.

Various organisations continued to make regular requests for use of the sports facilities. Among those accommodated were the Welsh Open Gymnastics Championships and international teams from Tonga, Australia and South Africa who were competing in the Rugby World Cup in 1991. The Sports Centre hosted the British Universities netball tournament and the British Universities Games (BUGS) in 1996. The latter competition attracted 500 athletes and a BUSA official commented that: "The people here in Swansea have done a good job. They have been friendly and accommodating throughout despite the Swansea weather bringing fog and torrential downpours". [14] The vagaries of the Welsh climate showed no consideration for sport but could not dampen the local welcome.

There were also continuous requests by individuals from the public to use the facilities as 'associate members'. The swimming pool was popular and there was no finer sight than observing a local eighty-four-year-old mother and her sixty-two-year-old daughter swimming lengths and performing 'perfect' rhythmical backstroke actions in adjacent lanes. When the daughter was asked if it was the swimming that kept her mother so fit and healthy, she replied: "Not totally, for every evening she also drinks a bottle of lager and smokes a cheroot."

The growing usage and increasing student numbers brought the need for further facility development and within financial constraints two squash courts and a storeroom were converted to create exercise areas branded the Tone Zone and Power Zone to enhance the provision of body-conditioning opportunities. Also, in 1995 a new synthetic grass pitch and floodlights was installed in the centre of the running track to replace the outdated and poorly-draining 'red gravel' area. This was of special benefit to the hockey clubs and other sports for matches and training.

However, the most significant facility development of the decade was highlighted in the University's Annual Report of 1998-99. Benefiting from National Lottery funding as described earlier, the report stated that: "In a triumph of cooperation between civic and higher education leaders the University has secured £8.5m of Sportlot funding to become home to Wales's new 50m swimming pool". [15] Further contributions of £1m each from the University and the city council were to be made towards the cost of the project. One of the driving forces of the project was the fact that both the University's and the city's swimming pools were ageing and in need of upgrading. Another was the growth of interest in competitive swimming.

The University's joint effort had fought off individual bids from Cardiff and Newport local authorities. As the decade ended with plans on the drawing board, 'partnerships and progress' were certainly in evidence. The move into the 21st century was to see even greater change.

CHAPTER FIVE

The 2000s and 2010s: new millennium and milestone ahead

THE 2000S OR the Noughties, as the first decade of the new millennium became known, was a time of conflict and incidents of terrorism around the world. Socially, in the UK, words and phrases like 24/7, credit crunch, pandemic and Facebook became broadly used. There was also the launch of Wikipedia and the smoking ban. Fashion included bleached hair and the hoodie while the Blackberry and the iPad were used more widely.

Sport saw outstanding achievements by individuals such as rower Steve Redgrave, boxer Lennox Lewis, athletes Kelly Holmes and Usain Bolt, swimmer Michael Phelps and golfer Tiger Woods. There were successful teams too as England won the Rugby World Cup, Liverpool FC the European Cup and Arsenal topped the Premier League undefeated.

British government policy had an increasing effect on universities, for Prime Minister Tony Blair and the Labour Party upped the entry target for young people to fifty per cent. Universal free higher education was to end with fees and student loans continuing from where they began in the previous decade. Confusion and debates arose about the purpose of universities. Were they for encouraging learning as an end in itself, or training places for the job market? A more 'business-like' approach was adopted for a more market-driven environment leading to greater competition in recruitment. Accompanying this was a desire for expanded, improved and attractive facilities.

Part of the social effect on students was the take-up of part-time jobs and the juggling of academic work. There was more commuting from home to University and less time (for some) to enjoy sport.

How did the above factors affect University sport? One striking acquisition came with the opening of the Wales National Pool. First Minister Rhodri Morgan performed the ceremony in 2003. It was a low-key launch and Commonwealth Games swimmer, student Steven Evans, was invited to swim the first length in the new pool. The versatility of possible configurations with the moveable boom, in addition to the warm-up pool and spectator seating, made it an eye-catching facility. Jane Draper was appointed general manager to be followed later by Jeremy Cole. Gary Rosser, the first full-time national coach for Welsh swimming, headed up the programming. He stated that: "Without a doubt the pool has had a major effect on performance levels". In 2007 the WNP was given Intensive Training Centre (ITC) status by the British Swimming Association (BSA). It was regarded as "an important development for the city and the University" and was to be one of only five such centres in the UK aimed at providing a "world class daily training environment". Experienced American coach, Bud McAllister, was appointed to direct swimming operations and he stayed for seven successful years until budget cuts by the BSA saw him leave to take up a coaching opportunity in Australia.

In 2003 the old University pool was closed. It had existed for over sixty years and held fond memories for generations of users. Good use was made of the structure for it was converted into a much-needed fitness centre (branded the Uni-Gym) with a range of cardio-vascular equipment and free weights. In the following year a sports injuries and physiotherapy suite was added. Within the city, the building of the new Liberty Stadium and the Morfa commercial complex saw a transfer of facilities to Sketty Lane and the adjacent King George V Playing Fields. These facilities included a new floodlit athletics track and grandstand, two artificial turf hockey pitches, six new tennis courts and an indoor training centre supervised by Andrew Griffiths. John Courtney was appointed grounds manager following Arthur Dahlgren who had served before him and Rose Fitzgerald took up the post of office administrator from Sarah Williams. Another Sportlot grant covered the facility developments to further cement the University's partnership with the city council. Both partners could take pride in the establishment of what was to become known eventually as the International Sports Village.

There were organisational and management changes at the University (and nationally) that affected sport. The local ones will be considered first. In 2003 the VC Robin Williams retired. During his tenure he had been a strong supporter of University sport. When praising his achievements, Peter Davies chairman of the University Council credited him with: "... the establishment of the burgeoning partnership between the city and the University". The fruits of this relationship were probably most vividly seen in the expansion of the facilities described above.

I also retired from my post in 2003 but continued working in a part-time capacity for another three years organising the PGCE physical education courses, delivering a sports science module and supervising the sports scholars. Gwyneth Diment was appointed head of sport, the University missing the opportunity to maintain the more appropriate position of director at a time when sport had reached a significant stage in its development. There was an adoption of a more business

The 2000s and 2010s

and commercial approach, perhaps mirroring what was emerging in the University at large. Gwyneth enthusiastically took up the reins.

Other agencies had a bearing on University sport, including the Welsh Assembly Government (WAG). Its first strategy for sport was outlined in 'Climbing Higher', published in 2003. [1] The strategy recognised that universities were prominent in sport academically and professionally, but little reference was made to the part they could play in elite performance. However, in 2004 Universities UK produced a document titled 'Participating and Performing: Sport and Higher Education in the UK'. [2] Its president, Professor Ivor Crewe stated that: "The role of sport ranges from world class excellence to community access and healthy living ... sport and higher education are engaging successfully to meet the aims of both higher education and sport ... performance sport is increasingly associated with higher education". This statement offered a good guide to the shape that Swansea was to take during the first twenty years of the new Millennium.

Further national developments saw the proliferation of sports scholarships and the Westminster government's decision to locate regional hubs of the UKIS at selected higher education campuses that in turn contributed to rising standards in the BUSA championships. In 2000 BUCPEA embraced further education colleges and a new organisation was formed called Universities and Colleges Sport (UCS). This body merged with BUSA in 2008 to offer a unified, stronger and national voice for University sport and the British Universities and Colleges Sport (BUCS) was founded. The launch of the new organisation involved MPs Andy Burnham and David Lammey, at the Houses of Parliament. Such prestigious proceedings gave a further boost to the standing of sport in universities.

At Swansea, successive AU presidents adapted to changes and dealt with issues such as the new Welsh Universities Cup

(WUC) that in part replaced the former UW championship in four sports. Other concerns were fundraising, Wednesday night sports socials, focus sports, websites, publicity, membership schemes, insurance, new charitable status laws and fairness for less mainstream sports. Sponsorship opportunities were sought for clubs and playing kits were soon embellished with sponsors' names and logos, moving away from traditional designs and mirroring the widespread commercial and TV influences seen in the Nineties. Veronica Short retired from her post as AU treasurer/secretary after over a decade of popular service, to be replaced by former AU president Richard Lancaster in 2001-02. Lancaster successfully turned his energy to addressing the above issues, promoting the AU and developing Varsity. In 2005-06 Bev Blackburn served a term as president after winning a tight election by two votes following five recounts. She was determined that the AU should celebrate the fortieth year of its founding by making the BUGS event, scheduled to be held at Sketty Lane, a successful affair. Later Simon Griffin brought what he described as 'boundless enthusiasm' to the role and energy enough to earn him a second stint as president. He promoted 'mega sports days' at Sketty Lane to support Wednesday afternoon fixtures. Griffin was also elected, as one of only four students, to the executive board of the newly-formed BUCS to help 'bed in' the organisation nationally. On leaving Swansea, he moved to Oxford where he enjoyed a role organising student sport.

How did student clubs react to the above changes and the wider sports environment? The WRU introduced regional rugby in 2003 and the performance of the national side ranged from wooden spoon winners to Grand Slam champions. The form of the University rugby club also fluctuated. In the SERC competition there were visits to Bordeaux and Cork. Despite missing injured former captain Sam Rees, they reached the SERC final played at St Helen's in 2002 but lost to French champions, the University of Pau. During the decade six future

The 2000s and 2010s

Ospreys and Welsh internationals came through the ranks – Tal Selley, Richie Pugh, (both also members of the Wales Sevens World Cup winning squad), Huw Bennett, Andy Lloyd and Jonathan Spratt. The sixth, law student Alun Wyn Jones (named Fresher of the Year in 2004) proceeded to a stellar career. He went on to captain Wales, the British and Irish Lions and became the most capped player in world rugby. Jones was made an honorary fellow of the University in 2014 and was later voted Welsh Sports Personality of the Year. He was awarded an OBE at the end of the decade in recognition of his outstanding achievements. He stated that: "The University and its facilities have been present in my life from a young age. Firstly, attending junior camps, as a student winning a Varsity match, as a pro for pre-season training, finally, getting my LLB." The rugby club also 'blooded' brothers Ben and Sam Lewis into the newly-formed Ospreys, while future Welsh international and Scarlet Rhys Priestland completed his degree at Swansea having previously studied at Bristol and Cardiff. Steve Mellalieu, John Bladen, Richard Lancaster and Alan Flowers took turns at coaching and developing teams during the Noughties and beyond. Lancaster moved on to Swansea RFC while Flowers took up the reins with the 'old enemy' and Varsity rivals, Cardiff.

The football club had a successful if eventful decade. At the beginning, captains Darren Braithwaite and Dan Swift were hard-working leaders. During the period, goalkeepers Andrew Greenwell, Mike Harding and John Chorley were dependable as the last line of defence, while Josh Collins, Laurie Inman, Richard Ryan and Jordan Pearson, amongst others, were regularly on the scoresheet. Both Harding and Inman served terms as AU president and Pearson also took on the role of match reporter. The 2002-03 season was outstanding as the 1st XI boasted a record that saw them win fourteen games and lose one. Under the leadership of captain-coach Chris Wells, the team achieved victory in the BUSA championship final beating Northumbria by 1-0, the first such victory for over thirty years. *Waterfront* described the occasion as: "... an emotional night at Buck's Head Stadium at Telford where Swansea University overcame all the odds to become the best University team in the UK". Well-led once more by player-coach Chris Wells, and aided by prolific scorer Richard Ryan, the club continued to have another run of good results in the following year. A *Waterfront* headline read: "Football fever as 1st XI reach final again". This time they lost narrowly to Loughborough. The next season under captain Stephen Healey the team reached the final for the third consecutive time and met Loughborough once more. A tetchy match ended in a draw at full-time but Swansea lost on a penalty shoot-out. During the tense aftermath of the game Swansea was accused of bad sportsmanship resulting in player bans by BUSA that affected selection for the following year. Relegations followed, then rebuilding. The students could well have profited with the services of Swansea City striker Guillern Bauza at this time. He was one of a clutch of the Swans' Spanish signings and had registered as a student, making him eligible for selection for the University team. However, Bauza chose to concentrate on his professional contract and his medical studies. His choice was rewarded with a first-class honours degree followed by a PhD that helped to secure his future after his footballing days. The decade ended brightly for the University when in Varsity: "a five-star Swansea beat Cardiff in style" to bring hopes of better times to come.

The rugby league club enjoyed a brief partnership with the newly-formed Celtic Warriors professional team based at Bridgend. Equipment and team coaching was provided by the Warriors for the students and membership of the University club doubled.

Men's hockey had three teams in BUCS competitions and weekend leagues. During the decade they won the Welsh clubs' shield competition on three occasions and the WUC final on penalty flicks when the Cardiff goalkeeper (according to a *Waterfront* report): "... moved like an elephant in quicksand". Due respect is offered to the metaphorical animal.

In women's sport, the netball club was well served by the Lawrence sisters early in the decade. The 1st VII won the inaugural WUC and were also crowned Team of the Year by the AU. The club had three teams in the BUCS championships and at the end of the decade celebrated a well-deserved win over Cardiff in Varsity.

Women's hockey also fielded three teams in BUCS. Danielle Selley, Gemma Petty, Polly Salter and Anna Lane stood out. Bev Blackburn and Kate Lloyd took turns as captain and the 1st XI won a promotion in the BUCS league. Anna Lane showed initiative and a determination to help others in less fortunate circumstances during the time of the facility development at Sketty Lane mentioned earlier. When the carpet-like synthetic grass hockey pitch was being replaced in the centre of the track, she helped enlist the assistance of the local Army Reserve Centre (along with transportation companies) to help stack the rolled-up sections onto lorries for conveyance by road and sea to South Africa. The pitch was relaid at Isandlwana for the use of school children with poor facilities for outdoor games. A plaque in recognition of the gift by Swansea University was erected on the site and has been favourably commented upon by tourists returning from the renowned 19th century Zulu War battlefield.

Women's football gained more participants, perhaps attracted by captain Hannah Mawson's mantra in 2001-02 that stated: "If you eat football, sleep football and drink beer, join the women's football club". Twenty-five new players answered the call enabling two teams to be fielded in BUCS and weekend leagues. In 2007-08 the 1st XI was voted the AU 'team of the year'. Players like captains Tasha Trotman and Nia Gape, along with American exchange student Laura Odino and Cardiff City Ladies player Sarah Johnson were mainstays of the club's success.

Women's rugby offered a mix of fun and serious play. On a tour to Amsterdam the advice from Emily Black was: "Stay away from the cakes" – cautionary guidance aimed at more than the possibility of putting on weight! A weekend sevens tournament in Bristol included: "… a hen party, camping in a paddock, 6am wake-up calls, noisy cows, consumption of 200 barbequed sausages, drinking games and hangovers". [3] However, throughout the era, performance was not neglected for Kath Leneghan, Aimee Jones (both Wales), and Fiona Britton (England) became international players. At the end of the decade, Siwan Lillicrap captained the club and went on to coach the team that won the WUC competition and gained runner up spot in the BUCS league. We will return to Siwan later.

Inclusiveness in sport gained a strong foothold and sport for the disabled was a fast-developing area throughout the country. From opportunities for the deaf and the blind after World War One, through to the post-World War Two pioneering work at Stoke Mandeville Hospital for ex-servicemen and civilians suffering with spinal injuries, progress continued. The 'sport for all' policy of the Seventies, the International Year of the Disabled (1981) and the first Paralympics at Seoul (1988) helped establish a pathway to world-class competition. During this time of development the University was able to assist in sport for the disabled on a case-by-case basis. Examples include a student athlete who was aided in his preparation for selection for the World Games for the Deaf in New Zealand and a wheelchair-bound member of staff who was given regular access to the swimming pool. Also, provision was made for blind and visually impaired cricketers to stage matches at the playing field.

On the international scene, Wales performed well at the Paralympics in Athens (2004) and Beijing (2008). Welsh athletes won thirty-one medals over the two games. By now the facilities at Sketty Lane had vastly improved disabled access. The WNP, partly due to inspirational coach Billy Pye, produced outstanding international disabled swimmers in Ellie Simmonds and David Roberts. The University had its own Paralympians in Liz Johnson, James Roberts and John McFall at Beijing. Roberts competed in adaptive rowing, finishing in fifth place, while Liz Johnson (who became a triple Paralympian) won gold at the 'Ice Cube' swimming centre. Newport-born, she went on to excel in many other swimming championships, took part in charity work, became a motivational speaker and was presented with an honorary fellowship by the University in 2015. Sports Science student McFall won a bronze medal on the track at the 'Bird's Nest' stadium and in showing delight with his success stated that: "I always had a list of goals and aspirations which didn't change after my accident, they just changed direction. Losing my leg has changed my life but it hasn't changed who I am". [4]

The WNP was proving to be a great attraction for students and the community. Following initial teething troubles, all water-based clubs were eventually accommodated on the timetable. Serious swimming and competition saw a host of medals won in BUSA/BUCS championships. At the end of the decade, the women's team gained second place behind Loughborough. International honours were awarded to Steven Evans, Dan Waddington, Bethan Coole, Georgia Davies, Alys Thomas and Meg Gilchrist who all represented their countries in Commonwealth Games.

Alongside the dedication shown by those above, there was fun too. Following a short course championship, a swimming club officer (allowing her mind to drift momentarily) reported that: "The tanned, toned, wet male torsos in nothing but Speedos walking around all day – I can certainly think of worse ways of spending a weekend". [5] Also, following a heavy water polo defeat by Cardiff a *Waterfront* article suggested that there should be an 'armband appeal' for: "… the University team desperately needs armbands to compete this year, so that it can float upright for the whole season, dramatically improving chances in matches. Please give generously". [6] Such 'tongue-in-cheek' remarks as those above help broaden the picture of sport to display its lighter side.

In Wales, people's interest in golf continued to grow and there was wide acclaim for Ian Woosnam again when he captained the Ryder Cup team to victory in 2006. There was much media coverage too of the build up to the 2010 Ryder Cup to be held at the Celtic Manor Resort. Alumni, including successful businessman Sir Terry Matthews (owner of the resort), Sarah Powell and Brian Davies (director of Golf Wales) along with First Minister Rhodri Morgan, (amongst others) worked together to ensure a successful tournament. The University golf team also adopted a more professional approach and at the beginning of the decade took part in 'warm weather training' at the David Leadbetter Golf Academy in Florida. The benefits were clear for on their return they won UW and reached the BUSA final for the first time before losing to Aberdeen. Wales international Tim 'The Swing' Dykes, as he was popularly known, captained the University team and lavish praise was bestowed upon him in a *Waterfront* article by one of his admirers as follows: "The golf swing is like a poem and in which case Tim can be described as the Dylan Thomas of the golf world". [7] During his post-University days, he joined the professional circuit. Other stalwarts of the club during the decade included Dave Gibson, Joe Evans, Jon Devereaux and Aaron Wilde.

Cycling was another sport with growing appeal. Inspiration in Wales came from Olympic gold medallists Geraint Thomas and Nicole Cooke. Various forms of the sport were followed and the University road racing team won the BUSA Peak District Hill Climb with Peter Greenwood earning first place. The Swansea cyclo-cross team were victors in the BUSA competition held at Singleton Park. They came in ahead of

Cambridge and Loughborough in a field of sixty riders. The tough weather conditions on the day did not deter the home team in what was described as a "mud, blood, tears and gears event".

Nationally, Wales had its boxing heroes in world champions Steve Robinson, Joe Calzaghe and Swansea's Enzo Maccarinelli. Interest filtered down into the University when a club was reformed after a lapsed period of twenty-eight years. Training was held at the Blaen-y-maes gym under coach Avoen Perryman in 2008-09 with the aim of entering BUCS competitions and attracting women boxers. The first aim was soon realised and the men defeated a strong Portsmouth team.

Exponents of the martial arts shone through in their various disciplines. Katrina Lowe and Rhys Jones won gold medals in the BUSA karate championships and Jonathon Jones was rewarded similarly in judo. In taekwondo, Will Hall represented Wales in the world championships and the University club was named AU Club of the Year in 2000. By the end of the decade Katie Franks (England) and Megan Davies (Wales and GB) achieved international honours.

Fencing was described as "high-speed chess with swords" and during the Noughties the men's team had a good record in Varsity, being undefeated over four years in epee, foil and sabre. Mike Loo, Matt King and Matt Bennett were mainstays of the club. The women were successful individually with Alysa Williams winning the UW championship and Lydia Johnson receiving a BUSA silver medal as well as being named AU Sports Woman of the Year in 2007-08. Rachel Rowles was an experienced GB international and a dedicated club member.

In racket sports there were some excellent individuals. The badminton club was well served by former Olchfa School pupil and Wales Commonwealth Games player James Phillips, Sohan Gadgit, brothers Darius and Barry Garnham, as well as Amy Genders. Francesca Lewis stood out in tennis, was positioned Wales's number one and earned a World Tennis Association (WTA) ranking. Later in her career she was elected Wales Coach of the Year. In squash PhD student, experienced and much travelled international Tegwen Malik, represented Wales in the Commonwealth Games in Melbourne.

Amongst the outdoor and adventurous activities, the University surfing club maintained its prominence. The ladies' team were BUSA champions in 2001-02 and their success was headlined in *Waterfront* as: "Swansea girls stand up for women's surfing". Kate Haile, Nikki Drakeford and Renee Godfrey made up the winning team. Godfrey, former Atlantic College student and daughter of Wales international swimmer Peter Godfrey, was also four times Wales surfing champion. After graduating in anthropology, she travelled to some exotic locations and became a TV nature researcher, director, producer, presenter and worked alongside Sir David Attenborough in producing the popular 'Planet Earth' programme. Explaining her love for surfing, she stated that: "Being a surfer gives you an obsession and addiction to the sea. It is a strong bond that drives me and leads me through life". [8] At the end of the decade, the women students were BUCS champions once more with Hannah Dixon, Seren Essex and gold medallist Beth Mason forming the team.

Other outdoor activities with increased appeal included rowing, riding and archery. The rowing club recorded its first win in Varsity and won £750 in sponsorship money from Gwalia Housing, to be spent on equipment. Daniel John and Kate Evans were selected for Wales. The club also won twenty-eight medals at the Welsh Indoor Rowing Finals putting their regular early morning training sessions to good effect. The riding club was based at the Cimla Equestrian Centre and members attended demonstrations at Pencoed and Hartpury as well as entering a BUSA competition held at Haverfordwest. The archers hosted the BUCS championships – the first Welsh University to do so – under the captaincy of Gary May. The club also gained fifth position in the UK Students 'online' league.

New sports appeared during the decade including American football, fin swimming, rounders, ultimate frisbee, kite-surfing, paintball and ten pin bowling. Also, the Swansea Sirens – a cheerleading team – was established. The Sirens adopted a dual role. They developed a club team for competitions and provided support and entertainment for University teams on big match occasions such as Varsity. They suffered some unwelcome experiences in their early days such as the breakdown of the music broadcasting system and being hustled from the field before completing their routines at a Varsity cup match in Bridgend. However, their presence and abilities soon became valued and appreciated as an enjoyable feature of the sporting atmosphere.

Alongside the clubs, intramural sport and voluntary recreational classes continued to attract students and staff. MWL football developed further and was fully covered by *Waterfront* with reports, results, league tables and scorers recorded. In 2003-04 Sports Science were champions and during the following year the competition was renamed UWS Football, bringing it closer within the administration of the football club. Exotic team names such as Sketty Bolognaise and Team Sloth, and leagues called Dylan Thomas and Lee Trundle, added colour. Also, sponsorship was secured in 2007-08 when the Walkabout Cup was introduced. League organiser Martin White stated that: "… the league is growing as a competition and social experience". Indoor five-a-side football, mixed netball and the Swansea Bay rugby sevens also remained popular.

As a result of the enhanced facilities, the number and range of fitness classes increased and early morning, lunchtime and evening sessions became available. Also, referral rehabilitation programmes were established at the Sports Centre in conjunction with Singleton Hospital for recovering heart and stroke patients from the community under the supervision of Kevin Harrison.

Another significant development during the decade that was to become an annual highlight was the growth of Varsity Day. Focusing on the charity Varsity Cup match between Swansea and Cardiff, the venues ranged from Cardiff Arms Park, St Helen's, the Brewery Field (Bridgend) and the Liberty Stadium. The matches attracted students, staff, alumni, sponsors, media coverage and wide public interest. In 2001-02 *Waterfront* described a change to the recipient of the charity funding – 'Varsity kicks Oxfam into touch' was the headline. The two universities had decided to support the WRU's Charitable Trust for injured players instead. Early in the decade, future captain Steffan Edwards, along with old Wellingtonians James Templeman and Peter Burroughs, earned Varsity man-of-the-match awards. Two of the latter's fellow former school mates, Kai Horstman and Jon Tenconi, were also prominent in University teams. In 2005 and 2006 Jack Dawson and Craig Voisey were winning captains and another victorious leader Richard Watkins summed up his experience as being a "brilliant day".

In 2001-02 the Charity Shield was introduced to engage more students. A greater number of sports was to be played during the morning and afternoon of the Varsity Cup match. This helped the day become: "... special to so many people for so many reasons" claimed a Shield competitor. In 2005-06 the Welsh Boat Race was initiated with Cardiff hosting the event at Cardiff Bay and Swansea choosing the Marina and the river Tawe for its venue. 2007-08 saw the awarding of caps being introduced for those who played in the Varsity Cup. Rob Evans (son of alumnus Gwyn who had starred in Welsh rugby during the Seventies) was captain that year and his team was the first to benefit from the new award.

However, greater numbers led to some 'over-enthusiasm' amongst supporters at Cardiff and it was reported that: "Rivalry tensions create problems at Varsity match". Provocative behaviour, trouble, fights and arrests took place. Blame was laid on the placing of anti-Swansea slogans on the scoreboard, ticketing problems, long queues for entry, and leaving pubs too close to kick-off time. By 2008-09, according to police sergeant Gareth Owen, officer in charge of operations: "... any problems that arose were minor". Excitement and incidents also occurred during the Shield competition as clubs showed a strong competitive spirit. Swansea's first victory in the Welsh Boat Race was earned in spite of a clashing of oars and a restart. The men's football 1st XI won their match in nail-biting fashion by 10-9 on penalties with goalkeeper David Cassidy making a dramatic save and then successfully converting his own penalty to secure a Swansea victory.

In 2009-10, following an absence of seven years, the student newspaper was pleased to announce that: "Varsity returns". The venue for the Cup game was to be the Liberty Stadium and the Shield matches were to be held at Sketty Lane. A crowd of 11,000 watched Swansea win the match at the Liberty. Captain Kerry O'Sullivan was presented with the cup by the Wales national coach Warren Gatland who remarked that: "It's my first Varsity and I have been very impressed by it. There is a great atmosphere, both teams going one hundred per cent and really enjoying it". [9] Varsity was overall turning out to be an eagerly-awaited, annual, successful and enjoyable occasion for the University community.

However, a less desirable feature amongst students took off nationally during the 2000s in the form of 'initiation horrors' that were associated with sports teams. Initiations had been part of society for many years with associated claims of 'bringing teams together' and making newcomers feel part of clubs. Nonetheless, linked with students, they often involved 'on the edge' activities and excessive drinking games. Some challenges involved 'pressure drinking' and nakedness. A *Waterfront* investigation revealed that students were often deterred from joining sports clubs because of some coercion to take part in ceremonies. There were conflicting views amongst AU club captains concerning the values of initiation activities. Some were more in favour than others. A captain of a women's club maintained that she: "... enjoyed getting involved with the initiations" but a men's team captain disagreed with the ceremonies claiming that: "... I think the boys initiated me ... there was three hours of my life last term that I can't remember and I will never get back". Consequently, excesses and tragedies at some universities led to student unions issuing bans on ceremonies. [10] Swansea had to keep a watchful eye.

Paradoxically, during the decade there was an increasing awareness of healthier lifestyles and the benefits of exercise. In 2005-06 a *Daily Mirror* survey result deduced that: "Swansea is the healthiest city in Britain". The British Heart Foundation (BHF) encouraged other cities to follow the example. It was thought that new facilities in Swansea (including the University's, the WNP and the city's revamped leisure centre LC4) coupled with the local parks and coastal location promoted a healthy attitude. [11] However, a wariness of the validity of the research should be adopted, for in 2004 a front-page headline of the *South Wales Evening Post* described Swansea as "Fat City" due to the unhealthy habits of its population. Nevertheless, a MORI research group finding revealed a better picture for student lifestyles nationally. Students were: "... going to the gym, keeping hydrated, swapping the pub for Pilates and staying away from the beer-swigging, kebab-munching stereotype in favour of a healthier lifestyle". An NUS report revealed too that: "A quarter of all students were teetotal, generally more active and interested in keeping fit than ever". Reasons given were financial (including the payment of fees, living costs etc) and holding down part-time jobs. Also, the more diverse nature of students, with eighteen per cent from overseas, many of whom were not attracted to the British drinking culture.

Student unions were adapting by converting bars to healthy food cafes and recommending exercise. Universities were also promoting healthy workplaces. [12] Such changes were in evidence on campus at Swansea. Also, it was claimed that less people were drinking in Wind Street during Wednesday night socials. Ironically this was leading to smaller bar profits, and consequent reduced sponsorships for the AU, resulting in detrimental effects on funding for sports clubs.

Students have a long association of support for worthy causes involving charity funding. This is often linked with physical challenges. Examples of these at the University were marathon running, distance fin swimming, fancy dress 'polar bear runs', a twenty-four hour boxathon and donations to the BUCS 'Right to play day'. Individuals, groups and clubs took part in these activities. Other more novel activities involved risqué calendar photo shoots following the example of the famous 'Calendar Girls'. One such shoot involved the men's rowing club at Swansea Marina where they stripped off and posed in line for the camera with only a strategically placed oar to protect their modesty. The caption above the photograph posted in *Waterfront* read: "Rowing club lads pose for all to sea". [13] It is not known how many calendars were sold.

The decade ended with the international standard facilities bedded in and management structures stabilised. Students and staff were enthusiastic about the new facilities and programmes of activity. The final decade of the centenary saw even more development that included a strong international connection.

2010-2020

THE YEARS 2010-20 brought the centenary milestone closer. The political scene in Britain saw Labour lose the 2010 election and the Conservatives gain power for the rest of the decade under the leadership of three different prime ministers. However, one successful Labour politician was Swansea alumnus Marvin Rees, a fleet-footed rugby player from the Nineties, who was elected to serve as mayor of the city of Bristol. The 2010s also saw the rise and fall of the UKIP party and the Brexit issue. A policy of austerity (with financial cuts) ensued that whittled away many places to meet and socialise with effects on physical and mental health. Lifestyles involved the omnipresent iPad and iPhone but numbers reporting loneliness trebled through lack of face-to-face contact.

The government's austerity policies impacted upon universities and funding turned into a crisis for many institutions. Deficits, competition for students, falling applications, strikes, job cuts and uncertainty regarding Brexit ensued. The system of student fees and loans was highly controversial and the growth in numbers was widely debated. It was argued that: "Universities should be academically difficult but financially easy". Swansea was not immune to the above but with a student population above 20,000 in 2016, recruitment was strong and the new Bay Campus was a flagship of the University's growing confidence.

What was happening internationally to inspire student sport? The 2012 and 2016 London and Rio Olympics and Paralympics were the most successful games of the new era for GB. There were outstanding performances from Mo Farah, Jessica Ennis, Chris Hoy et al. It was a golden era for Wales at the Olympics with eighteen medals won as part of GB teams or as individuals as Geraint Thomas, Tom James, Jade Jones, Hannah Mills, amongst others, excelled. Swansea University Olympians included local girl Georgia Davies, who had learned to swim as a toddler in the old University pool. She was selected for the London Games while Swindon-born Jazz Carlin swam in Rio where she was a double silver medallist in the 400m and 800m freestyle competitions. Richie Pugh, too, was at Rio coaching the GB women's sevens rugby team before later taking full responsibility for the Wales Sevens programme. Georgia Davies was an outstanding swimmer and amongst her achievements were winning gold medals at European and Commonwealth championships. Jazz Carlin, in addition to her Olympic medals and other successes, also won gold at European and Commonwealth level. While engaged in her business and accountancy degree studies, she claimed that: "I want to be fighting for medals, I don't just want to be making the team" – an attitude that helped her meet any challenges. At the end of the decade, another alumna, Swansea-based swimmer and Commonwealth champion Alys Thomas, was selected to be an Olympian and was a finalist at the Tokyo Games. At the same Games, the already-mentioned Fiji Sevens coach Gareth Baber earned a gold medal while GB hockey player, Jacob Draper, also competed at Tokyo. More will be written of him later.

There was success too for Wales Disability Sport on a worldwide scene with Paralympians Aled Sion-Davies, Mark Colbourne and Hollie Arnold achieving in their disciplines. Swansea University honorary fellow Tanni Grey-Thompson received a lifetime achievement award from the BBC. The University had its own Paralympians in boccia exponent David Smith who won three gold medals in successive Paralympics and was awarded an OBE in 2022. Engineering student Matt Whorwood and history graduate Gemma Almond competed in swimming. Whorwood won bronze medals at Beijing and London while balancing his academic studies well enough to earn a first-class degree. He claimed that: "Swansea offers so much with an outstanding pool, academic facilities, teaching and coaching. I enjoyed a work-life balance to meet the demands of training, competing and study." When asked about her ability to combine academic study and international sport, post-graduate Almond commented that: "Academia and elite sport are more closely related than people might think; a PhD requires a lot of commitment, the ability to set goals and targets in the short and longer term, a willingness to face set-backs and a passion for what you are doing". [1] Former

Sport and Exercise Science student James Roberts, who had competed in adapted rowing at Beijing, became a double Paralympian following selection for the sitting volleyball team at the London Games. His versatility saw him also compete internationally in swimming and wheelchair basketball.

The University was also prominent in two Commonwealth Games involving leadership, representation and success. Glasgow (2014) was Wales's most successful Games to date winning thirty-six medals. Alumnus Brian Davies (Sport Wales Director of Elite Performance) acted as Chef de Mission and was awarded an MBE for the inspiring part he played. In 2018 when the Games were held at the Gold Coast, Australia, Wales celebrated the most successful time in its history by finishing seventh in the table and winning ten gold medals. Swansea students and alumni who participated in either Games in a range of sports were swimmers Alys Thomas (gold medallist and record-breaker), Georgia Davies, Jazz Carlin, Alex Rosser, Ellena Jones and Hannah McCarthy; bowler Anwen Button; athletes Caryl Granville and Dewi Griffiths, and hockey players Jacob Draper and Ioan Wall. A contribution in which the University can take some pride.

Alongside the positive stories there were revelations of the darker side of international sport. Individuals like Tiger Woods, Oscar Pistorius and Lance Armstrong made the headlines for the wrong reasons. There were doping controversies in cycling and athletics with Russia being banned from international competition. Corruption and financial rule-breaking were highlighted in football and rugby while renewed concerns were raised about racism and athlete welfare. University sport did not escape incidents of anti-social behaviour and during the decade there were reports in *Waterfront* of sports people being involved in street-fighting, drunkenness, damage to transport on away trips, attempts at match-fixing and further undesirable instances of initiation ceremonies. A Students' Charter was introduced

The 2000s and 2010s

between the University and the Students Union in an attempt to regulate behaviour.

In 2012-13 a significant change in the University's sports management infrastructure took place. Due to the toughening of budgets, a vision for greater efficiency and a streamlining of SU and AU activities in conjunction with the department for sport and physical recreation, a new branding was introduced named Sport Swansea. The AU ceased to exist after a period lasting forty-six years. Dan Ryan-Lowes was to be the last president, but he was confident that: "... student sport would grow after him". The role of AU president was changed to that of a sports officer. Imogen Stanley was the first to be elected to the position. Under the new branding facility management, development, recreational programmes and sports clubs came together, reporting to a Sport Swansea Board. By 2010 there were forty sports clubs and these had increased to over fifty by 2020, all with their own management structures. Sadie Mellalieu took up the new position of Sports Clubs Manager with Rhodri Mugford liaising with BUCS fixtures and, along with successive elected student sports officers, helped to bed in the new systems. Charlotte Peters held the sports officer role for two years and endeavoured to reduce fees for students' use of facilities and raise the standard of match day conditions for clubs. Felix Mneck followed her and concerned himself with diversity in sports and identifying barriers that prevented participation. Robyn Lock was elected next. She was an outstanding rugby player who became a Wales international. Another rugby player, Gwyn Aled Rennolf, a founder member of Clwb Rygbi Abertawe, succeeded Lock and sought to improve the gym facilities at the Bay Campus as well as promoting the need for more floodlighting for playing pitches. Three women sports officers saw out the closing years of the decade. Sophie Hargreaves was a football and water polo enthusiast while Ffion Davies, who followed her, was a stalwart of the netball club. Georgia Smith was elected to see in the new centenary. She believed that she had: "... gained a strong understanding of the demands of the role" due to her experience as captain of the swimming club, participation in water polo and being a member of the executive board of Sport Swansea.

The year 2017 saw the retirement of Gwyneth Diment as Head of Sport. Gwyneth had held her position for fourteen years as part of forty years' service to the University. She made an enthusiastic contribution to all-round practical activities, showing particular interest in netball, squash, keep fit sessions and PGCE classes. Additional management commitments at the Sports Centre saw her embrace change in a positive and energetic way. Steve Joel, whose previous experience in sports administration included roles with Sport England, British Sailing and West Somerset County Council, took her place. Steve resigned in 2020 after driving interest in high performance sport and developing scholarships, while Kevin Harrison retired shortly afterwards. Kevin had conscientiously served the University for almost thirty years, managing the old swimming pool and its programming before the building of the Wales National Pool. He transferred his interests to 'dry-side' duties including overseeing health and safety matters, fitness developments, referral cardiac rehabilitation schemes for the public and staff supervision.

The nature of 'partnerships and progress' begun in the late Nineties continued, bringing further facility development; this time, with Swansea City FC, then a Premiership club. The University leased the Fairwood Playing Fields site to the Swans for the development of a state-of-the-art training facility. From 2012 the Fairwood site was transformed with the installation of top-grade grass and floodlit synthetic pitches, new changing rooms, sports science and rehabilitation facilities, at a cost to the football club of approximately £12m. At the official opening of the transformed venue, VC Richard Davies declared that: "We want to be able to offer our students an outstanding sporting experience with facilities fit for the 21st century ... It is a particular privilege to collaborate with a football club whose success has put Swansea on the global map". [2] The facilities were to be a tremendous boost to the University football club for training and playing, despite the fact that rugby and cricket could no longer be accommodated. The partnership with the Swans led to the University sponsoring the club and having its name and logo emblazoned at the Liberty Stadium in an effort to encourage student applicants.

Another (short-term) partnership development was that of the 360 Beach and Watersports Centre, a unique facility formed in conjunction with Bay Leisure Ltd with land released by the Swansea City Council. It was aided by European Union funding. At the centre, situated opposite the St Helen's ground, recreational opportunities became available for beach volleyball, football, touch rugby, paddle boarding and canoeing. A hospitable cafeteria facility helped make up an attractive leisure area.

One downside in relation to partnerships was the withdrawal of support for the elite Paralympic swimming programme by the British Swimming Association in 2013 due to financial stringencies. Athletes were moved to Manchester prior to the Rio Olympics which was a blow to disability swimming in Wales.

The University continued to provide its own facilities in response to developing trends and the need to upgrade. The Shed on the Singleton campus was a conversion from a former biomechanics laboratory to a dedicated strength and conditioning facility to be used by elite athletes and high performance sports teams. Fully furnished with the latest equipment and overseen by experienced coaches led by Gareth Beer, the facility was available from early morning to suit the training times of students around their academic work. The Shed complemented the Uni-Gym at Sketty Lane. The indoor climbing wall at the sports hall was also upgraded and was a welcome improvement for climbers and enthusiasts of the newer sport of bouldering. The Bay Campus provided for the physical activity needs of its students with a new multi-purpose sports hall, fitness room and outdoor areas for small-sided games.

It is not surprising that with the acquisition of such top-class facilities there would be requests to host training bases and events of a national and international nature at the Sports Village. In 2012 the Mexican and New Zealand Paralympic teams, along with the Irish triathlon squad were hosted prior to the London Olympics. According to Sport Wales: "... the successful hosting of events is seen as a prism through which people see and engage with us". With appropriate respective partners (for example, sports governing bodies, Swansea City Council, Sport Wales and WAG) a number of international competitions were successfully held at the University's Sports Centre with further support coming from campus accommodation, catering and other areas. In 2014 the International Paralympic Committee (IPC) European Athletics Championships were held at Sketty Lane, Swansea being the first UK city to hold the event. Over five days, 580 athletes from forty-nine countries took part with Russia, Ukraine and GB heading the medals table at the close. It was estimated that 20,000 people were involved in the games, including athletes, officials, spectators and visitors all enjoying "an atmosphere of strength, power and pride".

Such events as that above require meticulous organisation, largely built on the goodwill, energy and dedication of volunteers to take up specific roles. Indeed, much of sport today would crumble without the volunteer spirit. Pleas for people to help with events were made within and without the University and the local community was quick to respond. One such community volunteer was retired industrial metallurgist Haydn Chilcott from Langland. He recounted some of his experiences from the IPC European Games: "I didn't have

The 2000s and 2010s

a clue what I was letting myself in for and was even more clueless when I was given the task of acting as the attaché for the Netherlands team. I soon realised how good these guys were. In the party was the women's 100 metres world record holder Marlou van Rhijn, affectionately known as the 'Blade Babe'. The commitment and ability of all the athletes amazed me and I was treated to watching competitive Paralympic sports at their best. Whether it be wheelchair racing with Hannah Cockroft, shot putt with Aled Davies or men's sprinting with Johnnie Peacock, I couldn't believe that I was actively involved with all these guys. All of a sudden, I became a 'naturalised' Dutchman and was willing 'my team' on to win in every competition. My fellow attachés were doing the same for their respective countries." [3]

Also in 2014 the BUCS Annual Conference and Awards Dinner was held at Swansea attracting 400 delegates. BUCS president and Wimbledon tennis presenter John Inverdale, along with international rugby referee Nigel Owens, were the guest speakers at the dinner.

The European Touch Rugby championships were also organised for fifteen countries divided into men's, women's, mixed, junior and senior sections. England, Scotland and Wales topped the tournament rankings.

In 2016 the International Universities Sports Federation (FISU) Rugby Sevens Championships were next to be held and this event was the first universities world championship to be organised in the UK for fourteen years. Nineteen teams from fifteen nations competed. Australia won the men's competition and France won the women's tournament. It was declared that: "The successful bid to host this truly global sporting event is a great accolade for the University". Preparation for the tournament again included a request for volunteers and once more Haydn Chilcott stepped into the breach. This time he was given the role of liaison officer for the Kenyan team. Alas, he was soon out of a job as the Kenyans failed to turn up due to visa problems. With some relief he was subsequently appointed to a similar role for the Malaysian party. His duties included arranging coach transport from and to London Heathrow. Also, facilitating the purchase of telephone SIM cards for the animated Malaysians (who had not previously been to the UK) to keep in touch with family and friends. He adjusted meal times and diets due to their celebration of Ramadan and once more 're-naturalised' himself, this time as a Malaysian. Chilcott claimed that: "... at the end of the games I proudly walked with the team during the closing ceremony into the stadium at Sketty Lane with great pride, waving my Malaysian flag". He further summed up his experience as: "... absolutely fantastic and I thank Swansea University for making it happen".

In 2015 three Rugby World Cup teams were hosted for training at Sketty Lane, one of only a few venues in Wales with the requisite facilities. The teams from Canada, Fiji and New Zealand all praised the welcome and support they received. Indeed, star-studded New Zealand may have benefited most as they went on to win the World Cup final against Australia at Twickenham. Apart from Sketty Lane, the All Blacks management requested use of the local All Whites clubhouse at St Helen's for a private social evening for their team and staff. There, wearing another hat as president of Swansea RFC, I was able to offer words of welcome and relate some of the history of the ground and past visits by New Zealand teams. It was October 13th and at the end of my talk when I asked the All Blacks party what was the significance of the day's date, I got a blank response. I then explained that on that day in 1876 the first ever rugby match was played on the St Helen's ground. They all nodded appreciatively. I then asked what else was significant about October 13th and again got little response. This time I responded vigorously: "It's my birthday!" Whereupon there were loud cheers followed by a chorus of "Happy birthday" and I was passed a pint of beer to down. On reflection it was less intimidating than if they had performed an impromptu version of the Haka with me as their target.

Continuing with the global theme, in 2016 an International Day of University Sport (IDUS) was initiated. It was to be celebrated annually on September 20th and was proposed by FISU with endorsement from UNESCO. The day confirms the importance of sport in universities and the part they play in communities in consolidating and developing quality PE and sport education in the service of citizens – emphasising the benefits that the 'wholeness' of sport can bestow.

Apart from the staging of international gatherings, Swansea had its own annual highlight event – Varsity – that continued to grow, engaging larger numbers of athletes and supporters. Indeed, it was to become one of the largest student events of its kind in the country. In 2010-2011 the Varsity Cup was held at the Millennium Stadium, the first time that two University clubs had played against each other on the WRU's hallowed turf. Alumnus Alun Wyn Jones briefed the Swansea students telling them that in his view: "Playing here is like playing nowhere else in the world". Following victory Swansea captain Rhodri Clancy stated that: "I felt a mixture of apprehensiveness and excitement before the match". A crowd of 14,789 cheered on the teams. Two years later Swansea skipper Jon Vaughan enjoyed his experience and claimed that: "To play in front of 14,000 people in your national stadium and win is a fantastic feeling". In 2016 the women's Varsity rugby match was played at the stadium for the first time, resulting in a win for Swansea. During the decade the Varsity Cup was played at the Millennium (now Principality) Stadium five times and at the Liberty on three occasions. Varsity was promoted and covered by *Waterfront*, radio, TV, and sponsored over the years in turn by Abbey National, Accenture, St Modwen, Tata Steel et al.

As part of Varsity Day, the Shield competition grew from twenty-one sports fixtures to forty-three to include a select

Intramural Football XI and staff matches in football and netball. All this indicated a strong desire to be involved in the event. At Cardiff, matches were played at University and city venues as well as the Wales Institute of Sport (WIS). Swansea venues included Sketty Lane and the Bay Campus. All Shield matches were previewed and reported in *Waterfront* and well supported on the day. A large crowd helped create a heated atmosphere that saw the abandonment of the men's football in Cardiff in 2011-2012 while the beer queues and failing transport arrangements brought complaints by some student supporters at Swansea in 2015-2016. Swansea won the Shield for the first time in 2016-2017 but student Declan Murphy commented that: "He who wins the men's rugby wins the war", indicating the perceived importance of the evening Cup match.

Within a growing sports environment, the competitive spirit engendered by Varsity Day and rising standards in BUCS matches, Swansea improved its universities' ranking to eighteenth position. Some clubs raised their aspirations to compete at the top level of University sport and weekend leagues. A selected group of clubs was chosen to make up a High Performance Sports (HPS) programme. Rugby, football, swimming, hockey, netball and table tennis were those nominated. Generic support was provided for each club and individuals in the shape of athlete lifestyle management advice, coaching, sports science services, strength, conditioning and physiotherapy support and scholarships – all a refinement of what had been available during preceding years. Each club was also to be in partnership with a strong local community club or organisation and a governing body of sport. Additionally, there was to be an administrative board of students, University staff and appropriate local personnel for each club overseen by the University's head of sport.

The progress of the clubs involved provides both an illustration and justification for the HPS approach. The rugby club earned promotion to the BUCS Super League, the way being led by hard-working captains such as Jay Williams and Adam Thresher who strove to maintain high playing standards. History student Ian Williams moved on to Oxford and earned three blues, while Rory Thornton was capped for Wales. There was a return to St Helen's for 1st XV Super League matches – the ground where some of the University's early games had been played 100 years previously. The club fielded five men's and two women's teams under the leadership of head of rugby Siwan Lillicrap and coach Hugh Gustafson. Partnerships were established with the Ospreys and Scarlets regions. The men's and women's teams worked closer together as one club. From 2010-11 it was claimed that there were: "... more girls than we have ever had in the squad and a better structured training programme". Promotion to the BUCS Premiership, a tour to Beijing (along with the men) for a sevens tournament and a Varsity match held at the Millennium Stadium followed before the end of the decade. The latter experience was regarded as: "a huge step in the right direction for equality in University rugby".

From 2011 the football club (perhaps inspired and animated like the rest of the city by the elevation of the Swans to the Premiership) won a series of promotions in the local Swansea and FAW national leagues, narrowly failing to reach the Cymru Premier in 2020 due to a technical facility issue. The club played in the BUCS Premier, fielded seven men's and two women's teams, embraced the organisation of intramural football and successfully developed 'futsal', an indoor mini-football sport. Captains Zak Shayler and Pete Ockwell played leading roles along with enthusiastic alumni overseen by the head of football, respected coach Dafydd Evans who helped forge a partnership with Swansea City FC.

The standard of the swimming club and its base at the WNP has been well documented and, in conjunction with Swim Wales coaches Stuart McNarry and Hayley Baker, maintained high standards. The latter was chosen to coach the GB team at the World Student Summer Games at Naples in 2019.

The men and women hockey players joined forces with the local Swansea hockey clubs to form the Swansea Hockey Club with a view of enabling students to play at the highest level in both the BUCS and national club leagues. Promotions to the BUCS Premier and National Women's Premier League followed. Success in the south Wales leagues and being elected Sport Swansea Club of the Year added to the profile. The appointment of coach Gareth Terrett in partnership with Wales Hockey took the club forward following strong commitment during the decade from captains who included Chris Hacking, Pur Samra, Jonny Cardy and the free-scoring Rory Thorburn. The latter (son of alumnus rugby international Paul) had chosen a sport that his mother Ann had excelled in while a student during the 1980s. Towards the end of the decade, two outstanding players set the standard for the rest of the students. Former Ysgol Gyfun Gŵyr pupil Ioan Wall, the youngest player ever, at 16 years of age, to represent the Wales senior team, consolidated his place at international level and represented his country at the Commonwealth Games in 2018. His University and Wales team mate, Cwmbran-born Jacob Draper, went even further, gaining selection for the GB team at the Tokyo Olympics. Draper also earned a first-class degree in economics and on his time at University commented that: "Sport for me at Swansea was everything. I made friends for life, whilst also taking advantage of world-class facilities, which I believe are the reason I could and was able to turn professional straight from University."

The netball club fielded five teams in BUCS and the Swansea district leagues, established an association with Wales Netball and was voted Sport Swansea Club of the Year in 2017-18. The University table tennis club was supported by Table Tennis Wales (TTW), held joint training camps, received dedicated coaching and regular 'table time'. Sarah Mengistab and Tsz

Yan Nancy Yeh won silver medals in the BUCS women's doubles championship in 2019. Coach Matthew Porter was appointed to oversee the academy and promote the sport across Swansea and the region.

A further boost to the support of elite athletes and the HPS clubs was the inclusion of the University in the Talented Athlete Scholarship Scheme (TASS). Following the Bannister Report of 1996 TASS was launched in England in 2004 and was subsidised by Sport England to provide scholarships and bursaries for 16- to 25-year-olds in further and higher education. The scheme was restricted to English institutions only until 2018 when Swansea was included. "We are proud to become the first institution outside England to be awarded TASS Dual Career Accreditation. It builds on our strong sporting tradition and recognises the excellence of our teaching and student support," said Pro-VC Professor Martin Stringer. In response, TASS Director Guy Taylor stated that: "It was important for us to recognise those institutions who place precedence on their athletes' education". [4] Imelda Morrisson was appointed TASS co-ordinator at the University.

It was also a game-changing decade in terms of profile, popularity and perception for women's sport. Nationally there were strong individual and team role models. Encroaching upon what was once regarded as male territory, Nicola Adams (boxing) and Fallon Sherrock (darts) led the way. In 2019 at Gleneagles, 80,000 spectators attended over three days to watch women golfers play in the Solheim Cup. Interest in performance took precedence over gender. Crowds flocked to the Barclays Women's Super League football matches. The Manchester derby drew 31,000 spectators while Chelsea versus Tottenham attracted 27,000. There was increased TV coverage and the Women's Football World Cup semi-final in France attracted 11.5 million viewers. [5] Rugby was "seized by female hands and given the good shaking it needed". [6] The latter sport was promoted through the media and the values of the game became uppermost. The women's game was professionalised in England, France and New Zealand. Improving standards, a boom in participation and an emphasis on proper behaviours saw the inclusion of the sevens game in the Olympics in 2016. Appointments and elections to administrative boards of the RFU and the WRU and an increase in presenters and commentators on TV gave women more credence in football, rugby and cricket.

The above trends were reflected in the University during the decade. Former AU president Siwan Lillicrap was appointed head of rugby, a jointly-funded post by the University and the WRU. She also had the honour of captaining the Wales women's team. Siwan later became one of the first recipients of a new WRU contract when the game became professionalised for Welsh women players in early 2022 – a further groundbreaking achievement heralding a new era for the sport. Jasmine Lane became the first woman to referee intramural football matches and Sophie Hargreaves the first to oversee the organisation of the men's leagues. Eight out of ten elected AU presidents/sports officers were women. Across campus an annual Women's Day event was established to encourage the take-up of new sports. Further afield, former sports science student Michelle Owen was appointed as a Sky TV Sports presenter for football and claimed that: "I'm here on ability not gender". As previously mentioned, Sarah Powell became the first woman CEO for Sport Wales. Such is the progress of women's sport since the days when women's football was banned by the Football Association on members' pitches in 1921.

Throughout the 2010s established, revived and new sports drew support and saw success. Endurance athlete Verity Ockenden competed at indoor, track and cross-country meetings in Europe and America. She represented England and GB and was a BUCS medallist. The men's surfing team won the BUCS championship in 2013-14 when Rhys Poulton took

FACILITY DEVELOPMENT

The wet 'Red-gra'

Case for a new pitch early 1990s

New 'artificial-turf' pitch 1995

Fog at Sketty Lane 1996

Lifting the 'artificial-turf' 2005

Packing the pitch off to South Africa

The old pool 1940-2003

Emptying of the old pool

Conversion of the old pool to a Fitness Centre 2003

The new 50m Wales National Pool 2003

Aerial view of the completed International Sports Village c2००

The Shed S & C for elite athletes

The Shed

Transformation of Fairwood Playing Fields with SCFC 2012

Retirement of Don Lewis (centre front) 1994, with grounds staff

INTERNATIONAL EVENTS AT SKETTY LANE

IPC European Athletics Championships 2014

WC training venue for NZ , Canada and Fiji 2015

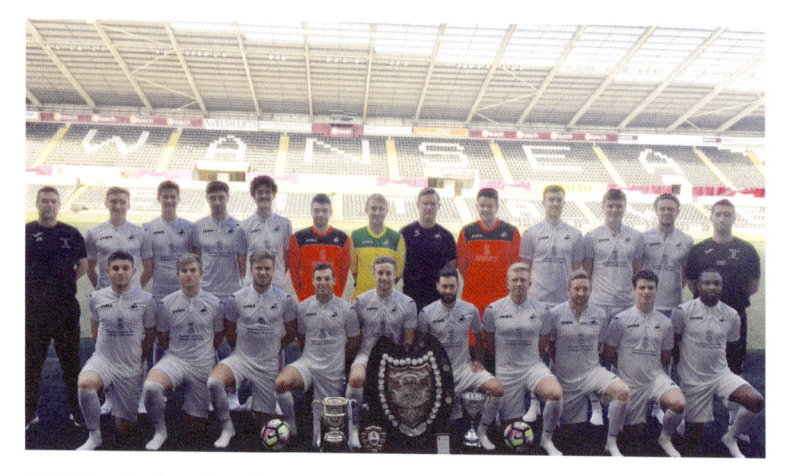

1st XI football at the Liberty Stadium late 2010s

Tae Kwon Do AU 'club of the year' 2000

Heineken Student European Rugby Championship Final

Wednesday 24th April 2002
Kick off 7.00pm
St. Helen's, Swansea, Wales

University of Wales Swansea
v.
University of Pau

£1

★ Heineken®

1st XV rugby SERC final programme.

Dewi Griffiths
GB athlete

Verity Ockenden GB athlete

Louise Whitehead Wales
AAA, BUSA medallist

Tsz Yan Nancy Yeh, Sarah Mengistab, BUCS table tennis silver medallists

Alun Wyn Jones and Siwan Lillicrap. 'Captains of Wales'

New Bay Campus 2015

Bay campus sports hall

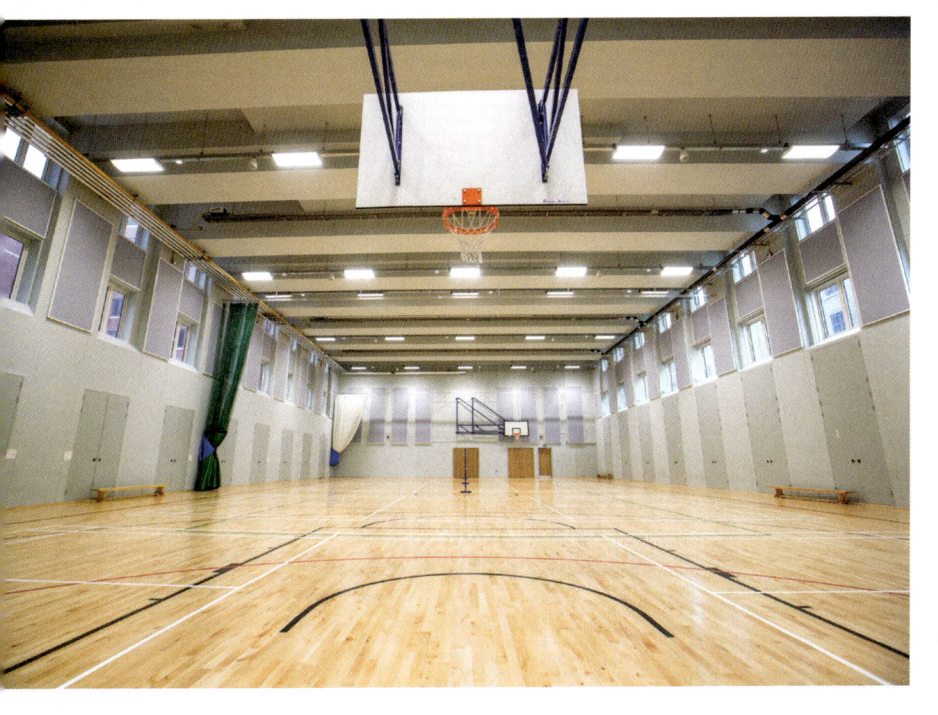

SWANSEA UNIVERSITY OLYMPIANS AND PARALYMPIANS

Howard Davies, Mexico City
1968 Athletics

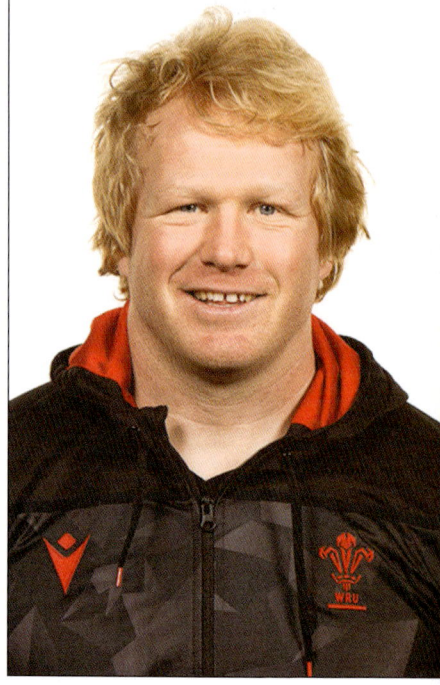

Richie Pugh, Rio 2016
Women's Rugby Sevens coach

Adrian Thomas,
Sydney 2000
Athletics coach

Ian Clingan, Beijing
2008 Sailing coach

Daniel Caines,
Sydney 2000,
Athens 2004
Athletics

Georgia Davies, London 2012, Swimming

Jazz Carlin, Rio 2016, Swimming

Alys Thomas, Tokyo 2020, Swimming

Jacob Draper, Tokyo 2020, Hockey

Gareth Baber, Tokyo 2020 Rugby Sevens Fiji coach

Liz Johnson, Athens 2004, Beijing 2008, London 2012 swimming

John McFall, Beijing 2008 Athletics

James Roberts,
Beijing 2008
Adapted Rowing,
London 2012 Sitting
Volleyball

Matthew Whorwood,
Beijing 2008, London
2012 Swimming

David Smith, Beijing 2008,
London 2012, Rio 2016,
Tokyo 2020 Boccia

Gemma Almond,
London 2012
Swimming

NEW SPORTS, PARTNERSHIPS AND BRANDING

American Football (Titans)

Swansea City FC shirt sponsorship

Swansea Bay Sports Park

the gold medal. Gwen Spurlock and Beth Mason represented Wales in the same sport, while at the end of the decade, Emily Williams won a BUCS gold medal. The windsurfers were also gold medal winners and Dyfrig Môn was selected for GB in sailing. The men's lacrosse team was promoted to the BUCS premiership and the American Football (Titans) team reached a national semi-final.

New sports like dodgeball, pole fitness, futsal, Clwb Rygbi Abertawe and kick boxing made their appearance. In the latter activity, the University could soon boast a European and World Championship winner due to the exploits of Llanelli's combative, cerebral Tennessee Randall. She became a student in 2016 and, alongside the demands of international competition, achieved a first in psychology, followed by a distinction in her master's. As a relatively recently-founded sport, full contact kick boxing does not sit within the Olympic programme. However, if and when accepted: "It would be an absolute dream for me," said Randall, who regards the sport as a great spectacle.

The boxing club was well represented in a Welsh Universities team against their English counterparts at an event held at the Oceana nightclub and the Swansea boxers won their Varsity match before a sell-out crowd at the refectory in Fulton House at Singleton. Boxers Josh Osborne and Ross Gwenter also won medals at BUCS championships.

Intramural sport and recreational classes saw their profile develop. The eleven-a-side football league obtained sponsorship, organised awards evenings, played finals at St Helen's and friendlies at weekends. Dan Newbury was an enthusiastic league chairman. The whole organisation was eventually brought under the structure of the University's football club. Five-a-side football leagues were held at the Bay Campus sports hall and the netball club promoted intramural sessions on Wednesday afternoons.

One hundred weekly fitness and wellness classes took place

at the Sports Village and Bay Campus where kettlercise, Pilates, spin and Les Mills classes appeared on the programme. Sports massage, physiotherapy and Health MOTs were also available and memberships open to the public.

As outlined, the final decade of the centenary saw the continued expansion of the University. Also, the development of particular areas of sport including facilities, the staging of international events, engagement with partners, additional scholarships and the greater involvement of women students. All this contributed to the promotion of elite, high performance sport and achievement. At the more recreational level as well, programmes broadened with the exponential growth of intramural sport and health and fitness classes.

However, apart from the expansion of the above, other distinctive activities developed too, and although already referred to briefly, are deserving of greater comment and recognition. These 'other areas' include staff participation, Post Graduate Certificate of Education (PGCE) courses in physical education, Sports Science degree courses and contributions to the sporting media.

Other sporting developments

Staff participation, PGCE (PE), Sports Science, Sport and the Media

Staff participation has always been prominent. Whilst the focus of the narrative so far has been mainly on the students, it was only natural that staff (academic, administrative and technical) should also show an interest in sports participation and offer support to student clubs where appropriate. The honorary position of AU staff treasurer was filled in turn by Dr Terry Williams, Dr Malcolm MacGregor, Roger Elias and Professor Phil Murphy. Other honorary positions were taken up in student clubs. Apart from those mentioned earlier in the rugby club, management science lecturer Bob Harris, geographers Gei Lewis, Pyrs Gruffudd, Graham Humphrys, along with alumni rugby players, Professors Rodger Wood and Ray Waters, always offered support. Historians Peter Stead and Huw Bowen did the same. Vice-Chancellor Robin Williams and pro-VC David Herbert took turns as president. Also, Professors John Baylis, Gareth Stratton and Mike McNamee became patrons while Professor Paul Preece was known to have furtively taken early leave from a Wednesday afternoon Senate meeting to answer a call for an 'emergency' referee to take charge of a BUSA match at Sketty Lane.

147

Community member and players' favourite Dai Matthews provided dedication, wise counselling and enthusiastic attendance at training and matches. He was known too for demonstrating singing prowess honed with his beloved Morriston Rugby Club choir.

Apart from taking part casually in forms of recreation, staff had their own clubs for tennis, squash, cricket, netball and football. Stalwarts in the various sports over the decades included mixed tennis organisers Helen Hodges and Mary Bodger, alongside lecturers Elizabeth Stead and Gwen Penny Evans. Amongst the men, tennis enthusiasts, enjoying relief from their teaching duties, were the industrious Alan Bodger and the dedicated Mike Shepherdson, Len Mars and Alan Evans. The ever-present David Herbert and philosopher Dewi Z Phillips, together with the competitive Malcolm MacGregor, James Davies and wine connoisseur George Evans, contributed to lively Wednesday evening club nights. Staff squash club regulars included Geoff Thomas, who also gave much support to the wider south Wales scene, and finance officers John Richards and Rhydian Morgan. Another ardent clubman was the combative classicist Eddie Owens, against whom I enjoyed many friendly challenges followed by equally satisfying recovery sessions at the local hostelry. The more temperate but equally determined Gwyneth Diment, Caryl Johnson, Judy Ganz, Liz Stone and Sarah Morgan were keen supporters of the women's game. Ceri Jones (football) and Beverley Evans (netball) promoted their sports in more recent times.

Down the years staff cricket was popular with a fixture list that included friendly and local league fixtures. Amongst the 'founding fathers' of the club were several from the English department. In the Fifties the side was blessed with 'old colonial' James Bartley, the debonair David Sims, and the wise Sam Dawson in the ranks. It is thought that Kingsley Amis drew some inspiration for his character Garnet Bowen in his novel *I Like It Here*, from conversations with his fellow staff

Other Sporting Developments

sportsmen about south Wales sporting culture. In more recent years, Professor Neil Reeve was a canny off-spinner and stylish stroke-maker. The swashbuckling Esmond Cleary and fellow economist Dave Blackaby were eager participants. Chemist Bill Bentley, all-rounders Phil King and Roger Owen, together with opening batsman Ken Stagg and Brian ('O Sole Mio') Cainen played a big part. Historian Kenneth O Morgan, (now Lord Morgan and a former principal of Aberystwyth) made regular appearances while Sir Glanmor Williams, Richard Docherty and Ernie Hinton all took turns behind the stumps. The registry's Matthew Sims (following in his father's footsteps), director of the computer centre Alan Gilmour, careers adviser Hugh Jones, and myself were among those who always looked forward to the annual UW staff cricket festival – what a team might be fielded if all those mentioned could be brought back together again! However, Jones regularly administered unsolicited career advice such as: "… don't give up the day job" if our thoughts ever fantasised about playing professional cricket. Nevertheless, the festival remained a highlight with overnight stays alternately in Bangor, Aberystwyth and Cardiff. The close on-field inter-college rivalry, camaraderie and post-match antics perhaps mirrored those of the students (which we all were at one time) in their inter-college matches during past decades. However, as the old adage states: "What goes on tour stays on tour".

A Staff Sports Week was inaugurated and driven by Huw Morris and Sarah Williams of the registry during the Nineties. It involved competitors from across University departments and eventually the lure of Varsity Day as an attraction saw the inclusion of staff teams. Staff entered intramural activities, joined in voluntary classes and families' sessions were also popular at the 'old' swimming pool and sports hall. Tony Ballantine, son of chemistry lecturer Jim, recalls some of those family times: "As a young boy I learned to dive by standing on the diving board with my toes curled around the edge and allowing myself to fall forward and plop into the pool. I found it great fun and I also played squash with my Dad who was a regular user of the courts."

Physical Education and Sports Science courses as fields of study are also justifiably deserving of mention as areas of activity. The attention so far has been on the majority of students, staff and alumni taking part voluntarily in a competitive and recreational manner and contributing to the community. Other areas of activity were courses of a professional/academic nature that were open to a more limited number of students. These included the Post Graduate Certificate in Education (PGCE) and the Sport and Exercise Science Degree. In conjunction with the education department optional courses in physical education (PE) had been offered since the 1930s alongside students' main teaching subjects. At Secondary level, the PE course initially entailed two hours per week. In the 1980s the course expanded to seven hours per week in University-based work followed by supervised teaching practice in schools. The main aim of the course was to equip students with the necessary teaching skills and enthusiasm to assist the school PE specialist. The optional Secondary PE courses attracted an average of thirty men and women students per year. From the 1980s a compulsory PE course of four hours per week was also provided annually for approximately 100 students preparing to teach in primary schools. These courses were supplemented with concentrated summer term activity weeks and national governing body of sport coaching award courses. As a result, many students took the benefits of their training as teachers into primary and secondary schools encouraging children to take part in sport and lead healthy lives. Regretfully for many, the courses came to an end on the transfer of the University education department to Swansea Institute of Higher Education (now University of Wales Trinity St David) in 2004.

Examples of alumni 'spreading the gospel' as teachers

include Haydn Davies a graduate (and University 1st XI cricketer) from the Fifties who taught mathematics and served the Essex Schools County Cricket Association for over fifty years, organising up to 100 matches per season. He was presented with an award for his services to schools cricket by former England captain Nasser Hussein, at a reception at Lords. Both Hussein and fellow England captain Alistair Cooke had benefited from Davies's enthusiasm for the game during their school days. [7] Another former Swansea PGCE student, from the Eighties, Oxford history graduate Derek Peaple, (winner of the education department's annual Ynys Seli Prize as the top student in the theory and practice of education) promoted the values of PE in his professional career. He became a headteacher at two secondary schools in Croydon and Newbury and proceeded to secure Specialist Sports College status for each school. He also gained a national award for an: "... outstanding contribution to education and sport" as part of the Olympic legacy of 2012. Peaple claimed that his: "... own passionate commitment to the all-round value of sports education was first kindled during my PGCE studies at University". [8] At a more local level Jeff Bird, PGCE mathematics and PE student (also 1st XV rugby captain), was appointed headteacher at Bishopston School. He enthusiastically drove forward a plan to regenerate the sports and leisure facilities at his school for the benefit of his pupils and the community.

The Sport and Exercise Science Degree scheme was introduced in 1997 following the interest in providing PGCE courses in PE. The new degree offered academic credence to sport, added infrastructure, attracted committed athletes and boosted student recruitment. Dr Simon Jenkins was the first course director. He was succeeded by Professor James Watkin and in turn Professor Gareth Stratton. Now based at the Bay Campus, the School of Sport and Exercise Science has a successful, wide and flourishing portfolio of undergraduate and post-graduate courses with staff engaging in teaching, research and assisting various sports bodies. From an initial cohort of seventeen students, numbers have grown to around 300. Many former students have also taken up influential positions after graduating. These include Huw Bennett who was appointed as a strength and conditioning coach for the WRU and Ross Nicholas the national performance director for Swim Wales. Tom Taylor gained a post as fitness coach to premiership football club West Ham United and Natalie Williams serves as an exercise physiologist for Sport Wales.

Sport and the media is another area of interest to which students, alumni and staff have contributed. Whilst the main thrust of this narrative has centred on practical involvement and performance in sport in its various forms, it would be remiss not to refer to the many who have subscribed to the understanding and enjoyment of sport through various forms of the media. Alumni and staff members have contributed through written, radio and TV forms of journalism to comment on and present sport. Some 'cut their teeth' by contributing articles to student newspapers during their University days as undergraduates before progressing in the industry. Others took up journalism on retiring from their playing careers while several with little involvement in the active playing side contributed through their sheer fanaticism and love for sport.

Examples of those with substantial experience throughout the years include Clive Gammon from Mumbles, an early 1950s student who for twenty years lived and worked in America as a writer for the famed *Sports Illustrated* magazine. He reported on sports other than the core American ones of football, baseball, basketball and ice hockey. He covered several Olympics, World Cups, reported on boxing and claimed a friendship with Muhammad Ali. During the early Eighties, Gammon flew from his base in New York to cover a Swansea RFC tour to California (on which I was coach to the All Whites) and I was able to offer some insight into the game which was gaining

Other Sporting Developments

greater prominence in the USA at that time. On his return to Britain, Gammon, an experienced angler, served as fishing correspondent for *The Times* and *Sunday Times*. Geoffrey Nicholson was another Fifties student from Swansea who wrote sports features for *The Sunday Times* and the *Observer* and worked closely with other eminent correspondents such as Chris Brasher, Hugh Mcilvenny and Peter Corrigan. In the Seventies, Martin Webster graduated in English and gained a PGCE but forsook teaching to join the BBC. He is credited with changing the face of televised track and field athletics. He worked at six Olympics and ten World Championships as a TV director and producer, earning a BAFTA for his outstanding professionalism. Fellow 1970s graduate Spencer Feeney was another local man from Waunarlwydd whose career in journalism saw him cover sport and become editor of the *Llanelli Star* and the *South Wales Evening Post*. Politics graduate Graham Thomas reported for the same evening paper as well as the *South Wales Echo* and the *Daily Mail*. He was also a presenter for the popular BBC Wales TV 'Scrum V' rugby programme. Andrew Gwilym wrote regular articles for the sports pages of the University's student newspaper before becoming media officer for Swansea City FC. More recently, classics graduate and England cricketer Steve James was appointed as a rugby and cricket correspondent for *The Times* and *Sunday Times*, while international rugby players Andy Moore and Dafydd James are frequent commentators on radio and TV. Further afield, former student rugby player Greg Thomas became senior media adviser to the Sydney Organising Committee for the 2000 Olympics and Rugby World Cups.

   Jason Mohammad, a Nineties politics and Welsh graduate, also an honorary fellow of the University, is a prominent figure on radio and TV presenting national snooker, rugby and football programmes and covering events such as the Rio Olympic Games and two football World Cup tournaments in Brazil and Russia. Of his time in Swansea, he stated that: "Being part of sports clubs was huge ... I didn't get to play for the cricket team, but I enjoyed the net sessions and wore the famous Swansea University training top with pride." Included in a new array of women sports presenters for Sky TV is the earlier mentioned sports science graduate and football pundit Michelle Owen. Her advice for those wishing to follow in her footsteps was: "... work harder than anyone else around you and be yourself".

Members of the University's academic staff have made notable contributions to broadcasting and sporting publications that offer a deeper understanding of the development of sport and its personalities. These include distinguished historians, Professors Dai Smith, Martin Johnes and Peter Stead. In the number of their works are Smith's *Fields of Praise* (co-written with Professor Gareth Williams), outlining the centenary of Welsh rugby. Johnes's *A History of Sport in Wales* offers an insightful examination of sport from 1880-2000. Amongst Stead's publications (co-edited with Huw Richards) is *For Club and Country – Welsh Football Greats*. All are highly respected additions to Welsh sporting literature.

As suggested, these 'other sporting developments' have also provided laudable contributions to the wide spectrum of University activity and beyond.

Conclusion

IN MOVING TOWARDS a conclusion, it is pleasing to see the centenary arrive on an ascending note despite the onset of the cruel and disruptive effects of Covid-19. From what has been written it is hoped that some appreciation and understanding can be gained of the nature and scope of sport in the life of the University during the past 100 years and the factors that have shaped it. In offering a glimpse into the future one might wish for more of the same with a vision of 'sport for all', continuing development, high standards and leadership in association with the community. Support for the promotion of HPS, the welfare of the 'scholar-athlete', the enhancement of facility provision, stable staffing structures and engagement with partners are all avenues of aspiration. Before the closing of the decade the new VC Paul Boyle enthusiastically displayed his interest in student sport from wet and windy touchlines. Indeed, as the centenary approached the University agreed to renew and increase sponsorship with the Swans and the Liberty Stadium, gaining widespread TV coverage as one of the benefits. Andrew Rhodes, Registrar and Chief Operating Officer, stated that: "We are pleased to be the front of shirt sponsor for Swansea City next season ... it brings huge benefit to Swansea University as we look to recruit students for the future. The relationship extends into our elite sports offering as well as delivering support for students and the local area". [1] The University is adopting what seems to be a national characteristic of the period – linking higher education with televised sport. Sponsorships of a lesser scale are also arranged with the Ospreys (now under the chairmanship of Monaco-based businessman, alumnus Robert Davies from Aberdare) and Scarlets rugby regions. Looking ahead there will be a growing use of technology to improve sports performance and the promotion of the Sport Swansea brand while embracing diversity, inclusion, equality, cohesion and values. The encouragement of HRE and wellness as a lifetime activity for the University community, within a mantra of 'no fun, no future', will be recognised as an antidote to some of the less positive sides of technology and daily demands. Much of the above is encapsulated in the University's new Sport Swansea 'Active University Strategic Framework 2020-23'. [2]

The seeds of this strategy were soon to sprout with the re-branding of the University's sporting base as the 'Swansea Bay Sports Park' and the declared intention to further boost facilities at the Sketty Lane/Ashleigh Road site. Thus hailing an exciting vision for the future.

There is evidence enough to suggest that the first 100 years have secured a place for sport as a vibrant and enjoyable part of University and community life for the next century. It is thriving both as a student activity and an academic subject. Finally, on reaching the centenary milestone the time is appropriate to celebrate the many who have forged and inspired the heritage of sport, those who are maintaining its traditions and others who seek to build on it in the future.

Abbreviations

AAA	Amateur Athletic Association
ACE	Athlete Career Education
AU	Athletic Union
BP	British Petroleum
BSA	British Swimming Association
BUSF	British Universities Sports Federation
BSSF	British Students Sports Federation
BUSA	British Universities Sports Association
BUCPEA	British Universities and Colleges Physical Education Association
BUCS	British Universities and Colleges Sport
CAB	Central Athletics Board
CCPR	Central Council of Physical Recreation
CCC	County Cricket Club
CEO	Chief Executive Officer
DFC	Distinguished Flying Cross
FA	Football Association
FC	Football Club
FISU	International Universities Sports Federation
GC	Golf Club
HPS	High Performance Sport
HQ	Headquarters
HRE	Health Related Exercise

IDL	Inter Departmental League
IVAB	Inter-Varsity Athletics Board
Inter-coll	Inter-college
IRB	International Rugby Board
LEA	Local Education Authority
MCC	Marylebone Cricket Club
MORI	Market and Opinion Research International
MWL	Mid Week League
NPFA	National Playing Fields Association
PE	Physical Education
PGCE	Post-Graduate Certificate in Education
Pro VC	Pro Vice-Chancellor
PTI	Physical Training Instructor
QAA	Quality Assessment Agency
RAF	Royal Air Force
RFC	Rugby Football Club
RFU	Rugby Football Union
R&A	Royal and Ancient Golf Club of St Andrews
SCW	Sports Council for Wales
SERC	Students European Rugby Competition
SRC	Students' Representative Council
SU	Students Union
S&C	Strength and Conditioning
TASS	Talented Athlete Scholarship Scheme
UAU	Universities Athletic Union
UW	The University of Wales
UGC	University Grants Committee
UKIP	United Kingdom Independent Party
UKIS	United Kingdom Institute of Sport
UNESCO	United Nations Educational Scientific and Cultural Organisation
UPFC	University Playing Fields Committee

Abbreviations

UWIST	University of Wales Institute of Technology
VC	Vice-Chancellor
WSF	Women's Sports Foundation
WIVAB	Women's Inter-Varsity Athletics Board
WNP	Wales National Pool
WRU	Welsh Rugby Union
WUC	Welsh Universities Cup
WWW	World Wide Web
YHA	Youth Hostel Association

Appendix

Some alumni with international, representative, miscellaneous and stand-out achievements
(Dates refer to student years or when they received their sporting honours)

Olympians
1960s
Howard Davies (athletics)
1970s
Adrian Thomas (athletics coach)
2000s
Daniel Caines (athletics)
Ian Clingan (sailing coach)
2010s
Jazz Carlin (swimming)
Georgia Davies (swimming)
Richie Pugh (rugby sevens women's coach)
2020s
Alys Thomas (swimming)
Jacob Draper (hockey)
Gareth Baber (coach Fiji rugby sevens)

Paralympians
2000s
Liz Johnson (swimming)
James Roberts (adapted rowing, sitting volleyball)

Appendix

John McFall (athletics)
2010s
David Smith (boccia)
Matt Whorwood (swimming)
Gemma Almond (swimming)

Rugby Union internationals
(Wales unless otherwise stated)
1920s
Watcyn Thomas (capt), Idwal Rees (capt), Claude Davey (capt)
1930s
Haydn Tanner (capt), Willie Davies
1940s
Alun Thomas
1950s
Bryan Richards, Ken Richards
1960s
Brian Davies
1970s
Phil May, Gwyn Evans, Mark Wyatt
1980s
David Evans, David Bryant, Paul Thorburn (capt), Andy Moore, Mark Bennett, Mark Schieffler (Canada), Eduardo Macedo (Portugal)
1990s
Andrew Lewis, Dafydd James, Dwayne Peel, Stephen Jones, Richard Smith, Ian Buckett, Rob Howley (capt), David Wetherley, Adedayo Adebayo (England), Andrew Williams
2000s
Tal Selley, Richie Pugh, Huw Bennett, Andy Lloyd, Jonathan Spratt, Alun Wyn Jones (capt), Rory Thornton, Rhys Priestland

Women's rugby union internationals (Wales unless otherwise stated)
Rhian Morgan
Natalia John
Fiona Britton (England)
Gee Fen Paw
Cara Hope
Katherine Leneghan
Sara Williams
Courtney Keight
Siwan Lillicrap (capt)
Elaine Skiffington
Alecs Donovan
Karen Williams
Aimee Price
Aimee Jones
Robyn Lock

British and Irish Lions
Haydn Tanner, Stephen Jones, Dafydd James, Gwyn Evans, Huw Bennett (coach), Alun Thomas, Robert Howley, Dwayne Peel, Alun Wyn Jones (capt)

WRU presidents
Hermas Evans, Gwyn Roblin, Alun Thomas

IRB chairman
Raynor Jones

International referees
John Gow (football), Chris White (rugby)

Stand-out football players
George Edwards (Birmingham City, Cardiff City and Wales)
George Renton (Wales Amateur XI capt)

Appendix

Peter Suddaby (Blackpool)
Mike Hooper (Liverpool, Newcastle)
Ronnie Goodlass (Everton and Fulham)

Commonwealth Games representatives
Bowls – Anwen Button
Swimming – Ellena Jones, Bethan Coole, Jazz Carlin, Hannah McCarthy, Georgia Davies, Duncan Rolley (England), Martin Davies, Steven Evans, Alys Thomas, Stephanie Watson (Scotland), Meg Gilchrist (Scotland), Dan Waddington (England), Victoria Hale, Alex Rosser
Rugby sevens – Gareth Baber, Richie Pugh, Tal Selley, Robert Howley
Hockey – Emma James, Sarah Powell, Jacob Draper, Ioan Wall
Squash – Tegwen Malik
Athletics – Howard Davies, Adrian Thomas (coach), Caryl Granville; Dewi Griffiths, Neil Horsfield
Weightlifting – Rhodri Thomas
Badminton – James Phillips
Admin management – JDB 'Jack' Williams
Chef de Mission – Brian Davies

GB internationals
Athletics – Alan Carter, Howard Davies, Neil Horsfield, Verity Ockenden, Daniel Caines, Adrian Thomas (coach)
Water polo – Ted Motley
Orienteering – Brian Bullen
Rugby league – Willie Davies
Swimming – Helen Walsh, Duncan Rolley, Georgia Davies, Jazz Carlin, Alys Thomas, Victoria Hale
Sailing – Ian Clingan, Dan Newman, Dyfrig Môn
Taekwondo – Megan Davies
Fencing – Rachel Rolls
Hockey – Ioan Wall, Jacob Draper

Wales hockey internationals
Daniel Jones
Ioan Wall
Emma James
Jacob Draper
Nicola Donald
Sarah Powell

Oxbridge blues
Hockey – Andrew Edwards (C)
Cricket – Steve James (C) Gul Khan (O)
Athletics – Nigel Greene (O)
Football – Peter Suddaby (O)
Rugby – Idwal Rees (C), Alan Prosser-Harries (C), Bryan Richards (C), Owen Jones (O), Ken Hopkins (O), Byron Light (O), Chris Dew (O), David Evans (O), Andy Moore (O), Simon Bryant (C), Andy Booth (C), Chris Clark (O), Ian Buckett (O), Gareth Baber (O), Richard Jones (O), Andy Collins (O), Paul Flood (C), Richard Dix (C), James Meredith (C), Neil Hennessey (C), Andrew Grabham (C), Ian Williams (O), Dilwyn Davies (O).

British Universities' representatives
Football – Graham Davies, Alan Hopkins, Robyn Jones, Phil Bowden
Water polo – Ted Motley, John Walters
Rugby – John Grice, Chris Lee, Alan Rees, Roy Lewis, David Protheroe, Gwynfor Higgins, Mark Wyatt, Byron Light, Brian Toms
Hockey – Joanne Ball, Alison Watts
Netball – Susan Price

Miscellaneous achievements
Steve Alexander (World power-lifting champion)

Appendix

Paul Russell (European surfing champion)
Andrew Hill (Irish surfing champion)
Zoe Lally (Irish surfing champion)
Renee Godfrey (BUSA and Wales surfing champion)
James Routledge (BUSA tennis singles champion)
Francesca Lewis (Wales tennis champion)
Louise Whitehead (GB Athletics World Student Games)
Nicola Donald (GB Hockey World Student Games)
Lesley Tyler (BUSF table tennis champion, Wales international)
Steve Jones, Will Davies, Steve Alexander (BUSF power-lifting champions)
Nigel Greene (Wales and AAAs athletics)
Steve James (England and Glamorgan County Cricket)
Gul Khan (Derbyshire County Cricket)
Scott Moffatt (Middlesex County Cricket)
Dan Cherry (Glamorgan County Cricket)
Mike Cann (Glamorgan County Cricket)
Adrian Dale (Glamorgan County Cricket)
Jo Crerar (England lacrosse)

Notes

Preface and Acknowledgements
1. McIntosh, P C: 'University Sport and Sport in General' – unpublished paper, FISU Conference, London, 1964

Introduction
1. Dykes, David: *The University College of Wales Swansea: An Illustrated History*, 1992, pp131-132

CHAPTER ONE
(1920s)
1. Dykes, David, op cit, p89
2. Mair, Alex: *Student Health Services in Great Britain and Northern Ireland*. Oxford, 1967, p5
3. Johnes, Martin: *A History of Sport in Wales, University of Wales Press*, Cardiff, 2005, p55
4. *Undergrad*: Student newspaper 1920 (Richard Burton Archives)
5. Ibid, 1921 (Richard Burton Archives)
6. University College of Swansea Inter-Collegiate Week Official Programme: 1925 (Richard Burton Archives)
7. Letter from Watcyn Thomas to College Registrar, 7th March, 1927 (Richard Burton Archives)
8. Mair, Alex, op cit, pp 6-7
9. Dykes, David, op cit, pp131-132
(1930s)
1. Johnes, Martin, p67

Notes

2. Dykes, David, op cit, p132
3. Dykes, David, op cit, p132
4. *South Wales Evening Post*, 'Pendragon' 13th October, 1932
5. Ibid, 19th April, 1933
6. Farmer, David: *The Life and Times of Swansea RFC: The All Whites*, Swansea, DFPS Ltd, 1995, p177
7. Rees, Jay: 'Centenary Essay: Making Beds With Envelope Ends, Beck Hall and Women's Experiences of Student Life at Swansea University 1920-1939'
8. Official programme, 10th Annual University of Wales Cross-Country Championship 1932 (Richard Burton Archives)
9. W Anthony Rees Collection 1937-40 (Richard Burton Archives)
10. Student Handbook 1937-38 (Richard Burton Archives)

CHAPTER TWO
(1940s)
1. Dykes, David, op cit, p132
2. *Dawn*: Student newspaper, May 1941
3. Ibid, March 1943 (Richard Burton Archives)
4. *The Guardian*, Obituary: 21st November, 2008
5. *Dawn*, 11th February, 1941
6. Match programme: Idwal Rees XV v University of Wales XV (Past & Present), Cardiff Arms Park, May 10th, 1947
7. Reflections: 'A Departmental Tribute'. June 1991, Education Department, Swansea University (unpublished).
8. Correspondence from Pauline Davies MBE JP, October 2017
9. *Crefft*: Student newspaper, 11th February, 1949
10. Ibid, January, 1949
11. Ibid, October, 1949

(1950s)
1. 'CCPR Sport and The Community – The Wolfenden Report', London, CCPR 1960
2. *Crefft*, 1st January, 1953.

3. Ibid, October, 1953
4. Ibid, March, 1951
5. swansea mumbler.com/latest/Swansea-University in the 1950s/class of 1954, 8th March 2020
6. *Crefft*, November, 1958
7. *South Wales Evening Post*, 11th December, 2019

CHAPTER THREE
(1960s)
1. Dykes, David, op cit, pp162-177
2. Dykes, David, op cit, p 205
3. *Crefft*. November 1965
4. *Western Mail*, November 1962
5. Correspondence from Anne Davies, April 2019
6. Ibid, April 2019
7. *Crefft*. 20th March 20, 1968
8. *The Times*. 29th February, 2020
9. *Crefft*. 2nd November, 1963
10. Ibid, 19th October, 1963
11. Ibid, October 1965

(1970s)
1. Dr Huw Jones, CEO Sports Council for Wales, Tribute to George Edwards, funeral-notice.co.uk
2. *Crefft*. December 1971
3. Ibid, December 1978
4. Ibid, February 1971
5. Ibid, April 1976

CHAPTER FOUR
(1980s)
1. Dykes, David, op cit, p213
2. Addicott, W S, 'The Development of Physical Education in State Schools in England and Wales from 1870 – 1920: A Sociological Study', MSc dissertation, University of Leicester 1995, pp90-94

3. *Double Take*, 27th January 1986
4. Ibid, 21st January 1985
5. Ibid, 5th May 1985
6. Ibid, 20th May 1983
7. Ibid, 22nd June 1984
8. *Bad Press*, 5th December 1989
9. *Double Take*, 4th November 1985
10. Ibid, 14th May 1982
11. Ibid, 3rd June 1981

(1990s)
1. 'Sport: Raising the Game', DNH, 1995
2. *Third Man*, 'University Education? Can't Beat It', July 1995
3. 'New Working Group to look at University Sports Scholarships', DNH, 176/95, news release, 11th October, 1995
4. Sport: 'Raising the Game. Report on University Sports Scholarships', DNH, June 1996
5. Sports Council for Wales Lottery Update, Issue 8, January 1997
6. *The Sunday Times*, article by Stephen Jones, 26th March 1995
7. *Western Mail*, 25th March, 1999
8. *Waterfront*, Student newspaper, 29th February, 2000 (Richard Burton Archives)
9. Ibid, October 1991
10. Sarah Powell, Business News Wales, 1st August, 2017
11. *Waterfront*, 27th October, 1998
12. Johnes, Martin, op cit, p103
13. The Sports Council for Wales 'News', 4th October, 1995, 'Women's Sport Needs Serious Treatment'
14. *Waterfront*, 12th March, 1996
15. Swansea University Annual Report to the Council, 1998-99, 'In the Swim'

CHAPTER FIVE
(2000s)
1. 'Climbing Higher', Welsh Assembly Government, 2003
2. Crewe, Prof Ivor, 'Participating and Performing: Sport and Higher Education in the UK', Universities UK, 2004
3. *Waterfront*, 5th June, 2002
4. McFall, John, *South Wales Evening Post*, 26th April, 2008
5. *Waterfront*, 4th November, 2001
6. Ibid, 22nd November, 2001
7. Ibid, 22nd November, 2002
8. Godfrey, Renee, 'My love of surfing inspired me to film Atlantic: The Wildest Ocean On Earth', BBC blog, 13th August, 2015
9. *Waterfront*, 4th February, 2002
10. Ibid, 22nd November, 2000
11. Ibid, 24th October, 2005
12. Ibid, 26th February, 2001
13. Ibid, 18th May, 2010

(2010s)
1. Gemma Almond, 'A Century of Aspiring Alumni', Swansea University (Marketing Dept), 2017
2. Vice-Chancellor Richard Davies, Fairwood Development, Swansea University (Marketing Dept), 24th July, 2012
3. Haydn Chilcott, Correspondence, 14th October, 2020
4. 'Swansea University Launch TASS Dual Career Accreditation Programme', Swansea University (Public Relations Office, 4th October, 2018)
5. David Walsh, 'Sky high viewing figures and record football attendances show women's sport has finally gone mainstream. But why has it taken so long?' *The Sunday Times*, 15th September, 2019
6. Stephen Jones, 'Women have offered reminder of the game as a force for good', Stephen Jones, *The Sunday Times*, 29th December, 2019
7. *The Times*, 'Modest East End maths teacher and Essex

Schoolboys cricket coach', (Memorial column), 25th April, 2020

8. Derek Peaple, Correspondence, 4th January, 2002

Conclusion

1. *South Wales Evening Post*, 'University takes over sponsor deal', 20th August, 2020

2. 'Sport Swansea: Active University Strategic Framework 2020-23' (Swansea University)

Bibliography

Richard Burton Archives Swansea University
Student newspaper collections: *Undergrad, Dawn, Crefft, Double Take, Bad Press, The Waterfront*
Annual University reports
Memoirs: 'Reflections – A Departmental Tribute – Education Department', (June 1991, unpublished)
Centenary Essay – Rees, Jay: 'Making Beds With Envelope Ends, Beck Hall and Women's Experiences of Student Life at Swansea University 1920-1939'
Correspondence: Pauline Davies (October 2017); Ann Davies (May 2019); Derek Peaple (January 2002)
Newspapers: *Western Mail, South Wales Evening Post, The Times, The Sunday Times, The Guardian*
Magazine: *Third Man* (July 1995)
Oral interviews: Cliff David, Prof David Herbert, Prof John Baylis, Don Lewis
Match and sports events programmes
'Sport: Raising the Game' (1995), Department of Sport and Heritage
'Sport: Raising the Game' (1996), Report of the Working Group on University Scholarships
'Climbing Higher' (2003), WAG
'Higher Education and Sport England', (March 2004)
'Universities UK' (2004): 'Participating and Performing: Sport and Higher Education', Prof Ivor Crewe
Sports Council for Wales: 'News' (October 1995)

Bibliography

Dykes, David – *The University College of Swansea: An Illustrated History*', (Stroud: Alan Sutton, 1992)

Mair, Alex – *Student Health Services in Great Britain and Northern Ireland*, London, 1967.

Johnes, Martin – *A History of Sport in Wales* (Cardiff: University of Wales Press. 2005)

Farmer, David – *The All Whites* (DFPS Ltd, 1995)

Holt, Richard and Mason, Tony – *Sport in Britain 1945-2000* (Oxford: Blackwell, 2000)

Addicott, W S – 'Sport and Physical Recreation in the Universities of England and Wales and the USA: A Comparative Study'. MEd dissertation (unpublished), University of Liverpool, 1979.

Addicott, W S – 'The Development of Physical Education in State Schools in England and Wales from 1870-1920: A sociological study'. MSc dissertation (unpublished), University of Leicester, 1995.

Illustrations

Acknowledgement is gratefully made to various institutions and individuals for permission to reproduce illustrations. Reasonable care has been shown to ensure that proper reference has been made to the originator of images. The author is thankful for the assistance in ensuring that this book is suitably illustrated.

Picture section 1:
The Richard Burton Archives (Swansea University); Swansea RFC; author's collection; Howard Davies; Wayne Stephens; Eric Bowers; Brent Mundy; Janet Wood; Haydn Chilcott.

Picture section 2:
The Richard Burton Archives; author's collection; Huw Morris; *Western Mail*; BUSA; Swansea University; *The Times*; *South Wales Evening Post*.

Picture section 3:
Author's collection; Swansea University; The Richard Burton Archives; Welsh Rugby Union; Howard Davies; Getty Images.

Acknowledgements

I SHOULD LIKE to acknowledge the assistance of various people who have helped to make this publication possible. Professor Hywel Francis showed a deep enthusiasm (tragically cut short), for recording many facets of the University's life and times. He saw sport as a definitive part of it and cajoled me into making this contribution.

I should also like to thank Professor Peter Stead for reading the early manuscript and offering sound advice and Professor Gareth Stratton for his interest and support.

The senior management of the University, the marketing department and alumni office were always supportive in responding to requests, as were former students and colleagues when approached. Siân Williams, Emily Hewitt and the staff of the Richard Burton Archives provided invaluable assistance.

I am indebted to the publishing company, Y Lolfa, and its excellent staff – editor Eifion Jenkins, for his meticulous attention to the manuscript, and in particular Robat Gruffudd, my longstanding friend, for his expertise and prompting. Diolch Robat!

Also, I am grateful to friends of the University and alumni. Amongst these are Mike James, Robert Davies, Roger Blyth, Stephen Hughes, Mark Rhydderch-Roberts, Mark Holloway, Phil Langstone, Gower Business Systems Ltd. and MGH Properties.

Lastly, but certainly not least, my wife Carole and daughters Ruth and Siân for their patience, advice and humour while what we affectionately described as 'the tome' was being compiled.